# The Heart of Buddhist Philosophy

NOLAN PLINY JACOBSON

Southern Illinois University Press
Carbondale and Edwardsville

Copyright © 1988 by the Board of Trustees,
Southern Illinois University
All rights reserved
Printed in the United States of America
Edited by Curtis L. Clark
Designed by Heidi Gunter
Production supervised by Natalia Nadraga

91 90 89 88     4 3 2 1

**Library of Congress Cataloging-in-Publication Data**

Jacobson, Nolan Pliny.
    The heart of Buddhist philosophy / Nolan Pliny Jacobson.
        p.  cm.
    Bibliography: p.
    Includes indexes.
    ISBN 0-8093-1396-0. ISBN 0-8093-1395-2 (pbk.)
    1. Philosophy, Buddhist. I. Title.
B162.J32 1988
181'.043—dc19                                                87-17376
                                                             CIP

The paper used in this publication meets the minimum
requirements of American National Standard for Information
Sciences—Permanence of Paper for Printed Library
Materials, ANSI Z39.48-1984. ∞™

*To Grace*

*in love and gratitude*

# Contents

# *Preface*

When it comes to understanding the philosophies of a people across the barriers of radically different linguistic and cultural systems, a bit of common street knowledge is the best advice: "It takes one to know one." Throughout its long history, Buddhism has been one of the world's systematic formulations of reality as a social process, with everyone and everything being related to everyone and everything else in what Hajime Nakamura and Daisetz Suzuki call "the interrelatedness of existence." Until the present century, efforts in the West to understand the world with the same intensity and depth as Buddhism were all dominated by Plato's "accent on form," the substance- and being-centered thinking of the Greek tradition. Heraclitus had carried out a brief revolution against such thinking, but his exalting of change was smothered until some of his insights were resurrected by Charles Darwin, Ernst Haeckel, Gustav Theodor Fechner, Étienne Boutroux, Henri Bergson, and Charles Renouvier, all of whom returned us to what James Wayne Dye terms "preanalytic modes of awareness."[1] Systematic elaboration of this process orientation was achieved by Charles Peirce, William James, John Dewey, Alfred North Whitehead, and Charles Hartshorne, providing for the first time in the history of Western philosophy insights giving us direct access to the Buddhist Way.

One of the leading physicists of our time, furthermore, indicates how fundamental the perspectives stemming from high-energy quantum physics can be in establishing a new way of thinking about our experience in the world. "If we think of the totality," David Bohm, writes,

*as constituted of independent fragments, then that is how
our minds will tend to operate, but if we can include everything coherently and harmoniously in an overall whole that
is undivided, unbroken, and without a border (for every border is a division or break) then our minds will tend to move
in a similar way, and from this will flow an orderly action
within the whole. The widespread and pervasive distinctions between people (race, nation, family, profession, etc.,
etc.), which are now preventing mankind from working together for the common good, and indeed, even for survival,
have their origin in a kind of thought that treats things as in-
herently divided, disconnected, and "broken up" into yet
smaller constituent parts.*[2]

It is clear that Bohm's kind of process thinking relates us directly
to the Buddhist view of the self-surpassing oneness of a world
that, in each fleeting moment, with its living moment-to-
moment manifestation of reality, is forever new. The world is
never the same twice; the universe is alive.

Most of the difficulties the West has had in understanding Buddhism are traceable to the lack of awareness of a fully developed
philosophy of process and the intrusion of attitudes and assumptions that make Buddhism as strange as the other side of the
moon. Illustrations abound. Drawing an object lesson from one of
the most prestigious Western scholars, we can see that there was
no way T. I. Stcherbatsky could understand either the Buddhist
view of the interrelatedness of existence (what Kenneth Inada
calls "relational origination") or a point even more central to Buddhist thought—namely, that what is really real is the living
moment, each momentary occasion of experience becoming a
part of the permanent past and contributing itself to the individualized, spontaneous, original, concrete experiences yet to come.
Stcherbatsky floundered on insights such as these merely through
the lack of a systematic process philosophy comparable to the
Buddhist system. "A dependent existence," he writes, "is no real
existence."[3] By emphasizing interdependence, Stcherbatsky
believes, Buddhism makes the momentary realities unreal, and
the Buddhist understanding of reality as a social process goes by
the board. The insight is hidden that the foundations of the world

are in these vivid, free, creative, responsive, original momentary occasions of experience, *to* which Buddhism seeks to return us, *from* the abstract, impersonal, thing-centered, being-oriented world in which all of us are reared. Buddhism urges us to probe our own individualized experience of the "cells of the universe," the momentary "really real things" in the "creative urge of the universe," as Whitehead puts it, "ever plunging into the creative advance." With Whitehead's insight that "we feel massively our present to be the product of the immediate past and the producer of the future" Buddhism heartily agrees in all of its different centuries and "sectarian" forms.[4] Stcherbatsky's presuppositions, however, placed him beyond the range of the conclusion of Henry Stapp, Ilya Prigogine, G. F. Chew, and other leading scientists to the effect that there are no mutually independent contemporaries anywhere in the world, that everything is related to everything else, that there are no self-established entities to be found.

Other object lessons can be found in the careers of Louis de la Vallée Poussin and Rune E. A. Johansson. "Until his final days," Inada writes, "Poussin could not completely divest himself from his Christian orientation." Poussin was finally forced to think of nirvana as the soul's experience of salvation.[5] This, by a scholar who, Guy Richard Welbon says, "devoted more time and writing to the meaning of the Buddhist nirvāṇa than had any European previously."[6] The substance-centered modes of Western thought prevailed in the end over the Buddhist denial of a permanent self *(anattā)*. The traditional outlook in which he was reared prevented Poussin from understanding, as it did Stcherbatsky, one of the central perspectives associated with Buddhism for twenty-five hundred years. The substance- and self-oriented enslavement to this traditional Western outlook is also found in another life-long European student of Buddhism, Rune E. A. Johansson. In his last major work, for example, Johansson denies the conventional notion of the "substantial self" but insists nevertheless on a "core of the personality," called *citta*, which is the "agency within the person which really attains nibbana [nirvana] and survives death."[7]

Only a systematic mode of process thinking, however, provides access to the oldest process orientation on earth. Buddhism established on a culturewide basis a new way of seeing and thinking about our experience in the world. In process philosophy, in either its ancient Buddhist or modern Western form, there is exposed the tension between what is concretely, directly, and spontaneously felt in immediate experience and the abstract constructions of reason and science. The aim of Buddhism is to alert men and women to the bewitchment of the intellect by the fictional self and by the ego-centered floating world with its compulsive drives and attachments. Buddhism seeks to rescue the creative energies of people from those anxiety-producing tensions, social coercions, and intellectual fictions that disorient men and women and render almost impossible the sense of the wonder of life.

James Dye expresses the one mental reservation readers may have with regard to the ability of Western process philosophy to open wide the doorway to the oldest international system of orientation and devotion. Process philosophy must show, Dye writes, "that it is the great alternative to Aristotelian substantialism, not merely by presenting itself as a different way to *think* about the world, but as the way the world seems to present itself for thought, and for perception and feeling."[8] In the systematic Western form of process thinking now accessible to everyone who can read, Buddhism does in fact become clearer to Western minds than ever before, inducing us to probe our most fundamental forms of awareness of the manifestly shareable world.

# Acknowledgments

The philosophers upon whose labors the present writing has rested are those who have lived on both sides of the Pacific Basin and who have sought to contribute to a deeper understanding of our life in the world. During the last century and a half, this philosophic labor has been intensified by turbulent changes sweeping over the most powerful nations as they reach for broader and deeper social unities and modes of communication. It is impossible for me to find words adequate to express my gratitude to the symphony of philosophers found in these pages. My indebtedness for this reason is best left to the documentation. The significance of these philosophers can best be indicated, however, by saying very simply that their insights are presently becoming unavoidable for rescuing humankind from the intellectual and cultural traps of the past.

The present book is primarily an invitation to readers to enter into direct communication with the small number of philosophers East and West—half a hundred at the very most—who have been most alert to the human failure that Whitehead calls the "fallacy of misplaced concreteness," the failure to be aware of the power of conceptual systems to hold men and women, as it has been said in Tibet, in deep sleep. The Buddhist contribution is formulated most clearly in chapter 4 in connection with the labors of Nāgārjuna, sometimes referred to as the Plato of the Buddhist tradition. The chapter has been read by Kenneth K. Inada, who has specialized on Nāgārjuna throughout his career. The chapter has been given its wider historical sweep by Herbert V. Guenther, both through his published writings and through his personal communications with the author. The contribution of Western philosophy to combating the "fallacy of misplaced concreteness" has been brought into focus in the work of Charles Hartshorne. In twenty-five centuries of philosophy East and West, Nāgārjuna and Hartshorne have performed similar historical functions: as rigorous logicians with a sharp sense for the nonlogical side of awareness, both have worked to loosen their traditions from the compulsive grip of prevailing intellectual commitments, Nāgārjuna freeing Buddhism from its ancient Upaniṣadic past, Hartshorne freeing the West from its long moorings in Aristotelian-Thomist thought. As compared with these two—Nāgārjuna and Hartshorne—philosophers past and present have struggled indecisively in the nets of language.

The insights constituting the central core of the book have been clarified by the recent studies of Heraclitus by Ken Maly and by the as yet unpublished writings of David Lee Miller, both philosophers at the University of Wisconsin at La Crosse. Both have fostered a clearer grasp of what I have learned from many years of reading Charles Peirce, William James, John Dewey, Alfred North Whitehead, and Charles Hartshorne on the philosophical traditions of the West and equally long preoccupation with Kenneth K. Inada, Herbert V. Guenther, Hajime Nakamura, and my Japanese colleague Seizo Ohe, all of whom are authorities in the traditions of the East.

The many people who have assisted me in my fieldwork in Burma and Japan must remain anonymous for the time being, though my friend Nyanaponika Mahathera, now president of the Buddhist Publication Society in Sri Lanka, should be acknowledged in this connection.

Words could never convey the deep gratitude I feel for the contributions of Curtis L. Clark to the form and content of this book. His labors have far exceeded the usual duties of even the most distinguished editors.

The indebtedness that is greatest of all, however, is to my wife, Grace, who continues to be the individual I have known who most fully embodies a sense of gratitude and reverence for the present moment and an ability to relate spontaneously to the wonder of life in the passing *now.*

*The Heart of Buddhist Philosophy*

# 1. Buddhist Philosophy on a New Human Frontier

*The great systems of Western philosophy all have seen themselves as dealing with something which has variously been termed Being, Nature, or the Universe, the Cosmos at large, Reality, the Truth. Into this state of affairs there recently entered the discovery that natural science is forced by its own development to abandon the assumption of fixity and to recognize that what for it is actually "universal" is process; but this fact of recent science still remains in philosophy, as in popular opinion up to the present time, a technical matter rather than what it is: namely, the most revolutionary discovery yet made.*

*John Dewey,* Reconstruction in Philosophy

Americans already have in their widest angles of awareness many of the insights of John Dewey and Alfred North Whitehead that enable them to understand some of the essential forms of thought in which Buddhism is presently finding itself at home. Writing from Burma twenty-five years ago, for example, I was so deeply impressed with what goes by the name of "pragmatism" in American circles that a chapter bearing the title "The Pragmatic Bent of Buddhism" appears in the book I was writing at the time.[1] Buddhist discussion groups in Rangoon, furthermore, were suggesting at the time that Whitehead's phrase "the aesthetic foundations of the world" furnished a striking parallel to the precise meaning of nirvana. It was an intuitive, unconscious flow of quality in the fleeting present that held the Buddha in a state of euphoria for forty-nine days, the Enlightenment with which Buddhism began.

Americans deserve, however, more adequate and specific information regarding the contributions Dewey and Whitehead have made to the philosophic outlook Buddhism is encountering on these shores. Together these two philosophers have had more impact on the American linguistic and cultural system than any pair of philosophers since the ancient Greeks. They have persuaded men and women to take a closer look at what is immediately given in their original, individualized, unthought, concrete experience and consider the possibility that this experience is their only direct and close engagement with life. Dewey and Whitehead stand together in opposing patterns of thought and action that obstruct new penetrations into the inexhaustible vastness of human experience, its connectedness with the rest of nature, the active energies passing from one particular occasion to the next. Both are opposed to the "trickle down" doctrines of "cultures of belief"[2] whereby individuals look outside themselves for the clues to the significance of their lives. Both consider, in Dewey's words, "the immediate existence of quality, of dominant and pervasive quality, as the background, the point of departure, and the regulative principle of all thinking."[3] Compared with the power of this qualitative flow in our experience, our forms of understanding are anemic, lacking solidity and life. Whitehead and Dewey stand together on this, that the aesthetic flow of quality through the perceptions, intuitions, memories, and aspirations of the live creature constitutes at once both a direction and a motivation for living.[4]

"There is in every individual," the Buddhist scholar K. Venkata Ramanan writes, "a feeling for the qualitative reality of events." "Unlike other creatures," Ramanan continues, "the human individual has a thirst to regain the dynamic, organic relatedness of which richness of life consists. To set free the sense of the real from its moorings in abstractions constitutes the chief-most mission of the farer on the Middle Way."[5] Buddhism carries out a frontal attack against the kind of ignorance that leads people to turn their backs on the quality of the passing moment, "complacently perched," as a recent book out of Sri Lanka has it, "on their cozy conceptual superstructures regarding the world."[6] It is doubtful if Buddhism's struggle against life's abstractness has ever found conditions more conducive to its acceptance and profound understanding than it finds in Dewey and Whitehead. For the length and scope of their careers, these two leading American philosophers labored to see more clearly the infinite fertility of human experience, insisting that rational principles and their institutional embodiments are justified only as they become searchlights illuminating more of the unthought and enhancing the vividness of individualized experience in everyday life. Rational principles become forms of *mis*understanding when they disinherit men and women from the flow of quality in the passing moment where individuals meet reality face to face. One of Whitehead's leading students at Harvard, Victor Lowe, comments that "we are so concerned with the fluctuations of fortune that we forget the perpetual aesthetic creation of each moment."[7] A Buddhist could have written that statement throughout any of the past twenty-five hundred years.

The major adversaries of Dewey and Whitehead alike have always been those philosophers who take their stand with the forms of cognition, ready to press them down upon all feeling of life's qualitative flow in order to make life seem more unambiguous, more lucid and secure than it really is. "Ultimately there are but two philosophies," Dewey writes; "one of them accepts life and experience in all its uncertainty, mystery, doubt, and half-knowledge and turns that experience upon itself to deepen and intensify its own qualities. This is the philosophy of Shakespeare and Keats." (Dewey here quotes Keats's famous letter characterizing men of great character as having remarkable capability for "being in uncertainties, mysteries, doubts, without any irritable reaching after fact and reason.")[8] The second philosophy runs in the opposite direction, seeking a secure refuge "variously termed Being, Nature or the Universe, the Cosmos at large, Reality, the Truth."[9] Dewey and Whitehead are the two leading American critics of the essentially logocentric, culture- and language-encapsulated, definition-minded philosophies of consciousness and cognition that have dominated the Greco-European tradition until the present time. Like Buddhists, they have built their perspectives of the human drama on the qualities from which most men and women spend their time running away—the originality, honesty, integrity, spontaneity, and depth that are already in our lives as life's unitary qualitative flow. Bergson said something that Buddhism, Dewey, and Whitehead could also have said: "On each individual nature in an immense inflorescence of unforeseeable novelty confers the absolute value of a great work of art."[10]

Whereas American philosophy has produced these two, along with a few colleagues and students over the last hundred years, Buddhism has been shaped throughout its long career by philosophers sharing this general perspective. Buddhism has been more successful than the West, moreover, in avoiding what has been called "the epistemological industry," emphasizing from the very beginning that what is needed is not a better theory of experience but to free experience from the facile artificial formulations of self-encapsulated, ego-aggrandizing cultures and peoples. Western history is strewn with misconceptions of the rich creativity of individualized experience in its qualitative flow. For Buddhism, all of these misconceptions have their source in the ego-centered, not-further-analyzable self whose deep unconscious compulsive drives are the source of the suffering Buddhism takes as its major problem.

Sharply critical of certain features of one another's thinking, as professional philosophers usually are, Dewey and Whitehead share one more thing in common. Both were working on what Dewey called "the reconstruction in philosophy" rendered necessary by revolutionary scientific discoveries, by a new American civilization based on communication of the original experience of its members, and by the global interchange between men and women previously shaped by the closed culture-worlds of the past. In both philosophers there is a heightened degree of sensitive awareness that to be reasonable in the new conditions of an interdependent world new forms of understanding are essential. Already during the period Dewey and Whitehead were working, millions of individuals were becoming capable of rethinking everything they had been reared to believe, breaking through the merely local, parochial, provincial ways and looking unflinchingly at evidence that corrects what they had "known."

In all of this there was no thought of providing conditions in which Buddhism would find itself at home. Neither Dewey nor Whitehead had any live interest in Buddhism; both, however, would have been pleasantly surprised to encounter the *Vajracchedika Sutra*'s phrase, "It is when one no longer believes in the beliefs of the self-interested and culture-bound self that the time has come to distribute gifts."[11] Both would have raised their eyebrows in agreement with this oldest international system of orientation and devotion for its belief in teaching individuals to doubt everything they have been reared to believe and to translate the forms of understanding into the actual world of the elementary qualities of everyday life, qualities that anyone can verify in his or her own experience, the "pure experience" Kitarō Nishida calls "the mundane ontology of everyday life."[12]

Whitehead was aware in a very general way of certain resemblances between his own thinking and "some strains of Indian, or Chinese thought,"[13] but of Buddhism in particular he harbored numerous misconceptions, such as the notion that Buddhism has a savior just as Christianity does, that the sense of active personal participation is discouraged in Buddhism, and that ultimate reality in Buddhism is centered in a Buddhist Absolute. Dewey, on the other hand, spent two years on a lecture tour in China and Japan, after which, as his daughter Jane remarked, "nothing was ever the same again." Strangely enough, Dewey felt more at home among the philosophers of China and Japan than he did among the academicians with whom he had taught for many years. In these thinkers he found reinforcement for his lifelong effort to understand human experience as immersed in the creative powers of nature. Dewey might well have written what Nishida had been saying: "The merely conceptual is not the real; the world of actuality is the world of self-creation, a creative world which goes on forming itself; we are all creative elements of a creative world."[14]

In China and Japan, Dewey was not only meeting philosophers who had been his students at Columbia University; he was also encountering a radically different way of experiencing the world. Among Japanese philosophers his lectures delivered at the Imperial University in Tokyo, published as *Reconstruction in Philosophy* in 1920, and many other Dewey books gave rise immediately to the John Dewey Society of Japan, still in existence, some of whose members earned more income translating Dewey's books than they received in their faculty salaries. Yoshio Nagano, for example, had more than thirty books on Dewey to his credit, a feat unmatched in any other nation. Nagano's 1923 thesis at

Tokyo Imperial University was a comparison of Kant and Dewey that concluded that Dewey's thought had replaced Kant's as the burgeoning philosophy of the modern world. It is plain that Dewey's thinking was congenial to Japan's Buddhist culture and its rejection of all absolutes and pragmatic bent toward the problems of everyday life, a culture that believes people acquire their sense of life's value, not from verbal instruction in the traditional beliefs, but from the feel of life's original spontaneous aesthetic quality in everyday life and from their sense of the interrelatedness of things.

Dewey and Whitehead, therefore, were changing the way Americans would eventually think about their experience in the world, but they were also opening new options for the entire community of humankind. Not only in America were the conditions being provided in which Buddhism would find itself at home. Buddhism's "new human frontier," as I have called it, was much larger than the American community; it was rapidly becoming the frontier on which millions of people lived throughout the globe. People entwined in hundreds of racial, ethnic, linguistic, and religious traditions were discovering that continuing in their parochial ways could bring all advanced civilization to an end. Against their will for the most part, members of these culture-encapsulated fragments of humanity were brewing in a global crucible the novel forms of awareness required for living in ever more inclusive wholes. Not only in America were people from ancestral cultures being forced to look for a cultural identity capable of embracing ethnic and religious differences without limit. The institutionalized patterns of the past were being caught up in a system of communication embracing the earth. Reflective men and women everywhere were recognizing the need to open themselves to their fellow-creatures or face the possibility of nuclear destruction. Leading scholars were saying that "the present time is probably the last time mankind will have the freedom to choose between life and destruction."[15] Buddhism could find itself at home under these planetary conditions, because under such conditions the suffering caused by compulsive clinging was raised to its highest degree, and this was the basic problem Buddhism had come into the world to solve.

An interdependent world of radically different levels of human development appears to have laid down a new condition for survival. The ability to relate, which has been the paramount principle of selection throughout the entire evolution of the human species, suddenly has become the everyday necessity for all. It is a time of appalling tragedy for millions in whom the capacity to relate has been dwarfed by the cultures in which they were reared. Relentlessly, the old limits of experience are being carried away in a flood of information communicated indiscriminately to everyone on the good earth, inducing the most sensitive individuals to question the beliefs and symbols of the ancestral order of life, something Buddhism everywhere has led people to do. It is more than a little amazing that this condition should be reproducing on the social level what Buddhism has taught in its concept of *pratītya-samutpāda* or *śūnyatā*—Nāgārjuna's "relational existence" on which, as T. R. V. Murti says, "the entirety of Buddhist philosophy turns."[16]

It is Buddhism's "process" or "nonsubstance" mode of thinking, as described in the following chapter, that fosters the ability to focus upon one of the central sources of human suffering—the deeper-than-conscious stress and conflict between what is disclosed in our unthought, spontaneous feelings and the abstract constructions of reason and culture. Buddhism through the centuries has devised forms of meditative thinking that bring out of the underground the nature of experience as originally given, prior to the intrusion of conscious thought. Buddhism has resources for assisting individuals to shift the focus of perception and memory to the natural rhythm of reality in its impenetrable depths. In the historical Buddha himself we see this endeavor to shift from the humanly contrived world, which compulsively drives its imperious laws into the very citadel of the human spirit, to something deeper than all cultural norms, something that can never become part of a humanly disposable world. This that is deeper—what the Buddha means by nirvana—is the consummatory experience of life: "Monks, there is a not-born, a not-become, a not-made, a not-compounded. Monks, if that unborn, not-become, not-made, not-compounded were not, there would be apparent no escape from what is born, made, compounded. But since, monks, there is an unborn . . . therefore the escape from what is born . . . is apparent."[17]

It is said that when Anaxagoras was asked why he preferred to be, rather than not to be, he replied, "In order to gaze at the sky and the harmony of the universe." Buddhism in all of its forms has transferred Anaxagoras's attention from the firmament of heaven to the aesthetic qualities of the passing moment where men and women find the ground of their individualized experience with which they were on the closest terms when they were very young.[18] It is these momentary nows, these concrete wholes in our original experience where we find our only direct, close, intimate, and spontaneous focus on reality, in comparison to which everything else is as distant as the stars. This is the way Buddhism, powerfully assisted by Dewey and Whitehead, can change the way people think about their experience in the world.

Philosophy has resources for fostering this change, but most of these resources are no longer in the European centers of Western civilization. As Charles Hartshorne says in his opening remarks to *Creativity in American Philosophy*: "To survey the resources of philosophy generally, one scarcely needs, any longer, to look across the Atlantic. There is somewhat more need to look across the Pacific, but there are competent Buddhist scholars among us also." A similar remark is found in the conclusion of the same work: "Somehow it is not for nothing that the waves of the Pacific beat upon one of our principal shores."[19]

# 2. Process Philosophies East and West

*There is growing evidence that the world is not just "out there" to be looked at by a detached spectator, but that the spectator is so deeply involved in his field of observation that at every moment he is a participant in what is going on. This involves a shift from objects to events, and from substance to process—from a mechanistic world view to a dynamic web of interacting processes. A process himself, man attempts to report on what has been, and still is, going on.*

*Herbert V. Guenther,* Kindly Bent to Ease Us

*One should not act or speak as if asleep. The world is one and therefore common to those who are awake; but each one who is asleep turns to a world all his own.*

*Heraclitus,* Fragments

Three times during the past twenty-five centuries, process philosophies have challenged the established intellectual and cultural membrane that interprets the meaning of human experience and value. Three times these philosophies have failed to rise to dominance, submerged by the prevailing ideas of the time and place. The first process philosophy to appear is associated with the teachings of Gautama Buddha in the sixth century B.C. Strictly speaking, Buddhism is neither a philosophy nor a religion in the ordinary Western meanings of these terms; it is, however, a method of awakening to what is really real in the world, a fact that could make it fit both Western categories, broadly defined.

The second process philosophy is found in the so-called fragments of Heraclitus (536–475 B.C.), "the weeping philosopher of Ephesus," the first of the precocious Greeks to place himself at the center of the social revolution of his time, just prior to the Peloponnesian War. The "fragments" are actually self-contained sayings designed for memorization in a community in which most people were unable to read. We should not think, therefore, that we have only the odds and ends of his larger work of continuous unfragmented prose; we have Heraclitus in a style derived from oral forms of communication, a style aimed at inducing people to accept a new way of life.

The third appearance of process philosophy, this time in a fully rounded-out and systematic form, came during what Max H. Fisch calls "the classical age of American thought,"[1] beginning about 1880 with William James and Charles Peirce and continuing to the eve of World War II in the work of Josiah Royce, John Dewey, and the Anglo-American Alfred North Whitehead.

At all three points where process thought was emerging, certain cultural dislocations were moving sensitive and perceptive individuals to shake off the ways their communities had sought to rationalize and justify the established order of life. At all three points, a universal problem that is not well understood even today came into focus: men and women everywhere live with a largely unrecognized tension, anxiety, and conflict between what is concretely and directly disclosed in immediate experience and the abstract constructions of reason and science. In every culture-world we know anything about, people are induced by the forms of custom and convention to turn away from their own feelings and aesthetic sensibilities. In their relatively underdeveloped stage of human evolution, people are easily persuaded that they must live by other people's notions, notions that everyone is pressured to believe, but as Zen has been shouting from the housetops for centuries, those who cling to words, letters, rules, conventions, and linguistic systems will never comprehend what any speaker is trying to communicate.

The philosophies of Buddhism, Heraclitus, and the American "classical age" philosophers all seek to reverse the claims of the linguistic and cultural superstructure and return individuals to their own deeper-than-cultural awareness of life's rich qualitative flow. All three philosophies remind us that even the most ingenious works of intelligence, once they have been institutionalized, have meaning that is microscopic and meager in comparison with the qualities found in the experiences of everyday life. All three focus attention upon the subliminal levels of experience, upon Whitehead's "tacit dimension" of the "deep experiences of organic existence,"[2] the fountainhead from which all the ingenuity and creativity of the human world are constantly watered. All three open the gates of quality flowing from the aesthetic foundations of the world.

Rationality is, of course, defined differently in different culture-worlds, and, indeed, even in the same culture-world at different times and places. From the vantage point of process thinking, a fundamental irrationalism infects the life-styles of humankind wherever the indefinite complexity of what is intuited and felt is forced into the procrustean beds of existing forms of understanding. Employed in ways indicated by process philosophy, conceptual form is a searchlight deepening understanding, probing the limits of awareness, opening experience to *more* of the variety and unspeakable qualitative richness of the world. As Kitarō Nishida puts it for the Japanese, "The merely conceptual is not the real; the world of actuality is the world of self-creation, a creative world which goes on forming itself; we are all creative elements of a creative world."[3]

The problem all three process philosophies bring into focus is the problem of how to interpret events that are deeper in human experience than any rational system can take into account, events that sweep over the physiological organism, shaking and dislodging old perceptual anchorages and bearing witness to feelings that are filtered out and lost when distilled through modes of interpretation presently in place. The fundamental stumbling block of life looms before us when these rules of logic and dominant forms of interpretation insist upon determining how and what we shall feel. This is the chief source of suffering in the human world. Individuals suffer and come face-to-face with nihilistic conclusions when no signs and symbols succeed in communicating the soft underside of the mind in the richness of its momentary now.

Process thinking, however, bears witness to the capacity of

human experience to be moved by a creativity that is deeper than the limited conceptual systems and cultural metaphors of a time and place. Not our thinking but "our experience," Whitehead writes, "sounds the utmost depths of reality." As he explains elsewhere, "Our lives are passed in the experience of disclosure. As we lose this sense of disclosure, we are descending to mere conformity with the average of the past. Complete conformity means loss of life. There remains the barren existence of inorganic nature."[4]

More fundamental than individual persons, social classes, linguistic systems, social institutions, and cultural metaphors is the succession of momentary nows, self-creative feelings that are emasculated and exploited by large-scale social organizations to keep human behavior within parochial and predictable bounds. Every social structure commits what Whitehead calls the "fallacy of misplaced concreteness,"[5] as each seeks to appropriate the concreteness of individualized experience for its own ends, fixing the attention of its members upon goals that, in the last analysis, generate the alienation from which the modern world for several centuries has been struggling, amid great suffering, to be free.

## Process Philosophy in the Buddhist Mode

"Buddhist thought," Herbert Guenther declares, "has always been process-oriented thinking. It is out of such a process-oriented view that Buddhism formulated its concern of being-with-others, suggesting a personal spontaneous experience in which we create ourselves and participate with our fellow-creatures in the creativity of the process we call life."[6]

Historically speaking, process philosophy first appeared with the Buddhist perception that everything is abstract but the present moment, the fulfilled *now* where we encounter life face-to-face as events coming into being and passing away to become part of the permanent past. Human suffering has its source in our compulsive clinging to each fulfilled moment as it passes, placing the obstacle of our compulsive drives before the creativity of life. The Buddha's teaching appropriates the traditional concept of "rebirth" to point to the forced transformation required for each fulfilled now to be followed by the next. Our proprietary attachment makes us prisoners of each present occasion, which we wish at times would last forever. Disoriented in this way, we are forcibly reborn from one moment to the next; in the interstices we stand outside what is really real. Individuals overcome this compulsive clinging through meditation and become part of the creativity of the world. Their identity from this point on is with the flow of quality in their experience, undergoing creatively what Rudolf Bultmann called "the eschatology of the moment," (thus giving Christian concepts of atonement and resurrection a new existential meaning).

Buddhism has taught for centuries that every moment has its own totality of conditions and causes owing to which it exists. These actual individualized moments are the final *real* things in relation to which everything else—persons, concepts, plans, purposes, and things—is a high-level abstraction. These moments are the happenings that constitute nature at large. In human experience each moment is, in Whitehead's words, "that portion of our past lying between a tenth of a second and a half second ago; it is gone, and yet it is here; it is our indubitable self, the foundation of our present existence." Out of these moments, as Hartshorne says, "we are creating something additional, however slight, in the mass of memories and bodily habits that make up character." These momentary nows are what William James calls "the living individualized feelings" in comparison with which the world of generalized objects is without solidity or life. We live forward in a risky and uncertain world, producing novel forms of togetherness as we move in the concreteness of a creativity which characterizes all matters of fact. The Russian scholar T. I. Stcherbatsky spoke directly on the issue elaborated in Whiteheadian thought: "A plurality of subtle, ultimate elements, technically called *dharmas*, creatively synthesize the past into the novel present, making the past an ingredient in the process of 'relational origination' forevermore."[7]

These passing moments, while the source of all motion through their creative synthesis of past and present, are part of the interrelatedness of existence Buddhism calls *śūnyatā* or *pratītya-samutpāda*. "The elements," Stcherbatsky writes, "co-operate and are in dialogue with one another; this co-operating activity is controlled by the laws of causation *(pratītya-samutpāda).*"[8] This pro-

cess of interrelated moments, producing novel forms of togetherness, is given a more detailed formulation in process philosophy
today, but it is *only* in Buddhism that human suffering is understood as having its source in an individual's inability to stay in
touch with these original concrete events given in the passing
now.

Beginning in the sixth century B.C., Buddhism has perceived
reality as the inexhaustible process of energy flowing out of the
depths of things, quite apart from any conscious effort to bring
the process about. Behind the first conscious moment of life, the
human organism has its own amplifying awareness of reality as a
dynamic, holistic process functioning mysteriously as life's pervasive ground. The process is infinitely creative. "It comes," Herbert Guenther writes, "and is there, eliciting a response precisely
by its being there." "A fundamental property of this inexhaustible
energy," Guenther says, "is what is termed in Tibetan records its
communicative thrust *(sngags)*, functioning as a coherent, unified
process."⁹ The real point in Buddhism is not to endeavor to grasp
this "thrust of the unthought" in a categorial system; the point is
to awaken to more of the vividness and vastness of experience
itself.

Kitarō Nishida, the first systematic Buddhist philosopher of
modern Japan and the most demanding thinker Japan has produced, is in fundamental agreement with the Tibetan point
Guenther has made. "Pure experience," as Nishida calls it, is the
root dimension in which reality presents itself prior to the intervention of sense experience or thought. It is this "pure experience" to which philosophy should be open, instead of imitating
the methods of mathematics and natural science. It is the fundamental fact that forms the immediacy of human experience; it is
*the* experience in which all others originate; it is reality creatively forming itself; it is the world of life.¹⁰

The ultimate facts in human experience are the concrete qualities or flashes of energy, the pure breath of our direct encounter
with life. These moments of the experienced now, according to
A. K. Warder, "are the elementary qualities which are not analyzable into anything else." This is something, Warder says, "that
anyone can verify for himself." A recent translator of Nāgārjuna
argues that even the poorest individual has an enormous unex-

plored capacity for awakening to these incommunicable qualities streaming through our everyday lives: "There is in every individual," Ramanan writes, "a sense of existence, a feeling for the qualitative reality of events, a sense of the ultimacy of the undivided being."[11] A leading work on Zen philosophy, furthermore, defines reality as the dimension of experience *before* it is analytically grasped through articulate words, as does "The Secret Oral Teachings in Tibet": "What has to be understood is that theories and doctrines of all kinds are the fabrications of our mind."[12] Everything in the Buddhist glossary is explained in terms of what is directly given in our original individualized experience, which is essentially "a revelation of our immediate contact with the world of dynamic flow and change."[13]

The one thing in the Buddhist orientation that is good without qualification, good everywhere under all circumstances, is the individual's awakening to the vividness of the passing now. The point of life is to increase, not our speed, but our responsiveness, our ability to be moved *before* any specialized zone of sense perception or anonymous routine can induce us to feel in socially mandatory or psychologically compulsive ways. Buddhism is thus an effort to relate us to the essenceless, selfless spontaneous stream of experience, to awaken us to what is always being disclosed in the momentary now. The primary task of Buddhism is to make it impossible for people to turn their backs upon this direct encounter with what is deepest in the human spirit. Other philosophies, to be sure, have had similar intentions, but they make our individualized experience more incomprehensible than ever by appealing to Platonic archetypes, Kantian transcendental egos, Hebraic-Christian souls, the emanations of a Neo-Platonic One, or other intellectualizations in the classical metaphysical traditions of the West. When we win a measure of freedom from the compulsive drive and the culture-encapsulated self, however, we discover the uncluttered, selfless, deeper-than-linguistic flow of individualized experience, drawing us into its concreteness, the mark of the reality in things.

In Buddhism even the gods one meets in the sutras are not deities in the Western objective sense, but represent mental states evoked by meditation, which may suggest new possibilities for a deepening and widening of our appreciation for the enormity and mystery of worlds beyond our ken. We are told by the new *Encyclopedia of Buddhism* that "Siddhārtha Gautama became the Buddha, the Enlightened One, as a result of a profound spiritual experience, an abrupt knowledge of Reality, which he realised under the famous Bodhi Tree near Gayā in northern India. This knowledge, being ineffable, could never be put into words; and all the verbal teaching of the Buddha was simply an indication or suggestion of its nature, a mere device for awakening men to real insight." "There is nothing in the teaching of Buddhism," Guenther says, "which our immediate experience does not contain."[14]

Unlike other creatures, the human individual is not confined to a biologically and socially determined nature: "He is not bound forever to his fragmentariness. He has a thirst to regain the dynamic, organic relatedness of which richness of life consists."[15] The ability to regain this organic relatedness is, however, the most underdeveloped feature of distinctively twentieth-century life. Only the rarest individual seems able to distinguish the raw, unformed flow of quality from the communal stereotypes in which he or she has been reared. The result is an almost totally subdued sense of conflict and tension between experience as concretely ours and the impact of cultural form, the tension and reality of this natural conflict being further concealed by an exaggerated fear of unshareable experience and a need to live with people who think and act as though they came from the same mold. In their voracious appetite for "belonging," people disorient one another from what is really going on. They satisfy one another's hungers, develop new industry, build cities of identical skyscrapers the world over, and never notice that all of it might strike a visitor from another planet as ultimately reducible to taking in one another's laundry.

Buddhism, however, has been functioning as a self-corrective method for almost twenty-five hundred years, freeing individuals one at a time from the deceits and disguises of the self-interested, class-oriented, culture-encapsulated self. Participating in disciplines of meditation and meditative thought, men and women become more creative respondents in the life they share with the speechless world's fellow-creatures. They learn that the universe is stranger and more beautiful than parochial stereotypes give anyone reason to believe. Following these meditations, people are liberated from the time-bound, authoritarian public models whose powers of control over human behavior now threaten the species with extinction. By teaching individuals to doubt everything they have been reared to believe, Buddhism fosters that higher form of reasonableness that enables them to translate what people are "saying" into the actual world of everyday life, rejecting what cannot be so translated. As David-Neel and Yongden quote from the *Vajracchedika Sutra:* "It is when one no longer believes in the beliefs of the self-interested and culture-bound self that the time has come to distribute gifts." And further: "It is the ideas which we hold, and not our material activity in itself, which constructs the chains that bind us."[16]

Out of the ancient Buddhist Way we are told, "No one can guide thee but thyself." "Do not put faith in traditions," the *Aṅguttara-Nikāya* says,

> *even though they have been accepted for long generations and in many countries. Do not believe a thing because many repeat it. Do not accept a thing on the authority of one or another of the Sages of old, nor on the ground that a statement is found in the books. Never believe anything because probability is in its favour. Do not believe in that which you have yourselves imagined, thinking that a god has inspired it. Believe nothing merely on the authority of your teachers or of the priests. After examination, believe that which you have tested for yourselves and found reasonable, which is in conformity with your well-being and that of others.*[17]

Nothing in the Buddhist orientation, therefore, has ever been an "article of faith" in the Western sense. Everything is to be analyzed and tested. It is only as we begin to doubt the validity of established institutions that we become capable of appreciating the ancestral order of life, valuing its achievements and perceiving its shortcomings in the long struggle of an evolving species. All the moral, political, and religious achievements of the past then become valuable resources to be used as probes for discovering more of the fullness and richness in the novel forms of togetherness in everyday life.

We are thus opened outward in the Buddhist perspective to a world that is wider than civilized form. What the conscious mind is fitted by cultural rearing to understand is the one-ninth of the iceberg in comparison with the eight-ninths submerged beneath the surface of life. An anthropologist appears inadvertently to be urging upon humanity the very recognition that Buddhism asks us to address: "One of the most significant facts about us," Clifford Geertz writes, "may finally be that we all begin with the natural equipment to live a thousand kinds of life, but end in the end having lived only one."[18] Human beings breed across ethnic and linguistic lines because everyone carries the conditions for birthing. Individuals can understand one another across cultural barriers because everyone has the capacity to become open to what is individually felt; even the most pathological conditions of anger, terror, and fear can bring people back to the common experiences of everyday life. People can become aware in apparently inexhaustible degrees; the capacity for being moved by others, and for responding to others, is inherent in awareness as such.[19]

Buddhism seeks to return the live creature, whatever his or her state of feeling and mind, from the dominant structures of conscious thought and institutional behavior to the concreteness that is forever nurturing human life. As Christmas Humphreys writes, "Buddhism lays stress on the individual and tends to attract all those who regard as evil the attempt of the State or any organization within it to shackle the minds of its members with dogma of any kind."[20]

Experience in its concrete presentness, in that vast background barely touched by conscious form, has always appeared to be of superior validity when compared with any concept or institutional form. As W. Howard Wriggins comments from Sri Lanka, Buddhists there have a predisposition "to be wary of the vested interests, the ambitions, and the presumptions of authority of man over man that are the inescapable accompaniments of human organizations."[21] Individual Buddhists in general do not seek their fulfillment in social institutions and social movements, all of which are viewed as monuments to the ego-trips of the disoriented few, because Buddhism has always struggled to keep experience in its individualized forms from becoming enveloped, Gulliver-fashion, in those ideological, metaphysical, and ecclesiastical structures that reduce awareness to the limits of the tribe, the social class, peer group, or profession. The Buddhist influence has always required the high abstractions of large-scale social organizations to be answerable to the living individualized now.

## Heraclitus

Amid the faulting of the institutional crust of ancient Greece, Heraclitus advanced what has been called a "terrifying perspective, resembling an earthquake in which everything seems to sway."[22] For the second time in the history of the human world a process philosophy emerged on the continental divide where experience in its inexhaustible creativity and richness was being overlaid by, as Nietzsche says, "the customary, the small, and the common, filling up all the crannies of the world like a heavy atmosphere everyone is condemned to breathe."[23]

Nietzsche can think of no one who more fully embodied this individualized experience of the vastness of a more-than-human world than Heraclitus. Among prose masters of Greece, Heraclitus is Plato's only equal, Nietzsche believes, a philosopher of unsurpassed power and originality, "like a star without an atmosphere." "As a man among men," Nietzsche adds, "Heraclitus was incredible,"[24] refusing to believe that people have an incurable need to receive from an outside, more reliable source the clues regarding the meaning of their own experience. Though an aristocrat by birth, accustomed to a society that ruled by intimidation, Heraclitus scoffed at the suggestion that people live better when they submit their individualized experience to be molded and subsumed under the conceptual metaphors dominant at the time. "To live successfully," he writes, "the world one thinks must be one's own, sharable but not borrowed from others."[25]

It is the greatness of Heraclitus, according to Heidegger, that he includes the "unthought" and thinks of being as "the process of disclosure." Every new insight that reaches conscious awareness originates in this unthought, often remaining in the soft underside of the mind for long periods, without being able to break through the barrier set up by the organized structures of conscious thought. Heraclitus realizes that, as Kenneth Maly says, "thinking's thought has a fundamental and originary bond to the unthought; the unthought demands to be heard and dealt with, thrusting itself upon us; *the thrust of the unthought is then the issue for thinking.*"[26]

Process philosophy is not just a different way of thinking about our experience in the world, nor is it, in Marx's sense, primarily a way of changing the world. For Heraclitus, James Wayne Dye argues, "it is the way we are led to think about our experience when we see the way the world presents itself for thought, for perception, and for feeling." The "weeping philosopher" grumbled that people "turn their backs to that with which they have to deal continually, and most of all, that which they encounter daily appears strange to them."[27] A kind of blindness is thus acquired, preventing people from seeing that, according to Maly, "the main issue is to wake up and teach wakefulness to one another." Every human being when healthy and whole lives with openness to what is being forever disclosed, because, Maly argues, "man cannot remain hidden (how could he?) from the unthought."[28]

In Heraclitus, experience is freed from the intellectual and institutional lock and key. Experience is interpreted by him in its own natural rhythms, as Dye believes, "rather than in terms of pure forms given to a consciousness supposedly capable of disinterested spectatorship." "In the most concrete sense," Dye continues, "there are no independent non-changing entities. All things are in process, and nothing stays as it was. Objects conventionally identified by a single name are really always changing."[29] Heraclitus also visualizes the world, according to Karl Popper, "not as an edifice, but rather as the totality of all events." And the experiencer is within the process, part of the universal change, rather than outside as a neutral observer. "The greatness of this discovery," Popper says, "can hardly be overrated."[30]

Process philosophy, however, died out in ancient Greece when the social turbulence mounted to intolerable levels, culminating in the Peloponnesian War, which lasted twenty-eight years, to be followed by the puppet government of the Thirty Tyrants in Athens, during whose eight-month rule as many citizens were killed as during the final ten years of the war.[31] The Heraclitean vision of a universe of dynamic creative forces working as a self-explanatory ground of change failed to resolve the cultural conflicts that were carrying the Greeks beyond the intellectual and social horizons of the traditional city-state. It was one among many efforts of brilliant philosophers constituting what has been called the Golden Age, an effort "to wake up and teach wakefulness" to fellow-citizens whose expanded trade with the whole Mediterranean world was bringing not only new commodities but new ideas and values that called into question the old parochialisms and taboos.

Following Heraclitus, those Karl Popper refers to as "the Great Generation" created the fountain from which Western civilization has continued to draw its ruling ideas, but several centuries of social and political turmoil followed, thrusting rational argument from the center of the Athenian stage. The cosmopolitan world of Alexander the Great tossed three continents of radically different culture-worlds into a single community in which citizens, resident aliens, and strangers from abroad would dwell together on equal footing and view one another as citizens of one world. The ideal was too new and too lacking in broad social support to become deeply rooted in the Mediterranean world. The voice of Plato was extinguished even within his Academy; Skepticism prevailed almost immediately following his death in the very place where the claims of the Patterns and Archetypes had been the topic of the day. The successors to Aristotle in the Lyceum forgot his original teachings almost in their entirety; his famous manuscripts were hidden to keep them from "barbarian" hands, until Sulla in 86 B.C. confiscated the entire library and took it to Rome.[32] In some circles mysticism came to the fore and new religions and philosophies were born: "Materialistic and positivistic attitudes toward life lost ground, and Platonism came into its own again with the appearance of the Neo-Platonic system of Plotinus—monistic, transcendent, emanative, with a theory of knowledge, ethics, and aesthetics based on ecstasy. But most fruitful of all in its consequences was the rise of the Christian religion."[33] A new period in the history of the Mediterranean world had begun.

## Process Philosophy in Its American Mode

After centuries of philosophical activity within the limits of the substance- and being-centered Greek tradition, Western philosophy, in the form of those Max Fisch designates "philosophers of America's classical period," has given many of the central perspectives of process thinking, including Buddhist process thinking, their clearest and most systematic formulation.

Charles Hartshorne, the major representative of these philosophers in the contemporary world, has, for example, related the corpus of this American tradition to what he calls "the oldest of the great international systems" in the most specific ways. Historians of the future, freed from the parochialisms that obstruct our view, will probably see that Hartshorne's major accomplishment has been his weaving of his own realization that experiencing is in principle creative together with Dewey's "logic of qualitative thinking," William James's radical empiricism and pluralistic universe, Royce's beloved community of interpretation (in *The Problem of Christianity*), Peirce's analysis of nature into events rather than things, and Whitehead's actual entities, prehensions, and creativity to arrive at a systematic formulation remarkably expressive of Buddhist thought. In Buddhism and in American philosophy, as summarized by Hartshorne, one finds the same emphasis upon the infinite fertility of human experience in a world whose creativity is its most universal feature, upon the centrality of dynamic change and the consequent inconclusiveness of all knowledge and speculation, and upon the diversity of ways in which individuals experience what is most real and the danger of imposing abstract categorial systems on the individualized and original experience of everyday life.

On numerous occasions Hartshorne has expressed our need to break free from the astigmatisms of Western thought. "I think it is time," he writes, "that at least the Buddhist tradition should be taken seriously into account. I have argued for years that there are indeed non-European ideas that can serve our European purposes better. It is notable that one (somewhat Americanized) European philosopher, Whitehead, has arrived, probably independently, at some central Buddhist insights, and that two Americans, James and Peirce, partly anticipated him in this." Buddhism is, Hartshorne says, "the greatest international alternative to our Judeo-Christian tradition; we can no longer ignore it." And further: "Our provincial neglect of this great tradition is out of keeping with the global responsibilities of our time."[34] Throughout his long career he has been endeavoring to make Buddhism a factor in American thinking.[35]

There is no major Hartshorne writing that does not relate some idea or concept at the core of his philosophy to what Buddhism has taught in all of its divisions and "schools." Illustrations abound:

> *Ancient Buddhism and Whitehead agree, against Aristotle, and also against Bergson, but in nearer agreement with Plato's* Timaeus, *that concrete reality consists of momentary actualities that successively become; this succession being what we call change.*[36]
>
> *If we are looking for concrete definite unitary wholes of reality, we should recognize that the individual-now is always a new such whole. The Buddhists, whom Peirce admired, saw this.*[37]
>
> *The momentary experiences are the primary realities and these do not change, they simply become. The "soul" or the self-identical ego is merely the relatedness of experiences to their predecessors through memory and the persistence of various qualities or personality traits. The first great metaphysician in the West to hold this view clearly was Whitehead, in the present century. To see this is the beginning of wisdom in the theory of selfhood. . . . The Buddhists saw it long ago. There are profound ethical and religious implications of this view which Buddhism appreciated and Whitehead also emphasizes. Egocentric motivations essentially consist in metaphysical confusion. This is why a Buddhist termed the egocentric view "writhing in delusion."*[38]
>
> *One should admire the genius of Buddhism in seeing into the complexity of this matter so long ago. It is not the ever-identical self that thinks or feels, now in this way and now in that; this self never thinks or feels at all, for it is an abstraction, and what actually has thoughts or feelings must be concrete.*[39]
>
> *As a college sophomore [in 1916] I learned from Royce's great essay on "Community" the most essential metaphysical lesson of all, perhaps, a lesson the Buddhists had learned long before. This was to detect the element of illusion (or, if you*

*prefer, confusion) in the idea of a plurality of selves mutually external to each other.*[40]

In the light of illustrations such as these, it is now possible to see Hartshorne as the great connective link between Buddhism and a group of American philosophers who are not surpassed in any nation during the past century, if, indeed, they have been equaled in the history of philosophy taken as a whole. No one but Hartshorne in the West has ever matched Buddhism in its emphasis upon the chiefly evocative role of reason in sharpening our focus on the soft underside of the mind, whose fugitive moments of rich and intense quality provide each individual with his or her direct encounter with life. Not even Buddhism has excelled Hartshorne's struggle to awaken men and women to depths and ranges of awareness for the enjoyment of which our potentialities have barely moved beyond the most primitive range. Hartshorne speaks like a Buddhist in arguing that what we experience in the present moment is the fundamental reality, in comparison with which all else is an abstraction.

This convergence of philosophies separated by thousands of miles and years, and by radically different cultural systems, stands unmatched in the history of the species. The strange upsurge of process thought in Western civilization, strange in the light of the West's cognitive bias and almost hypnotic fixation with theoretical structure from the time of its emergence among the amazing Greeks, could probably not have happened at all without the concurrence of three remarkable transformations in the intellectual and cultural atmosphere of the United States, where modern process philosophy in its systematic formulation—best represented by the thinking of Charles Peirce (1839–1914), William James (1842–1910), Josiah Royce (1855–1916), John Dewey (1859–1952), and Alfred North Whitehead (1861–1947)—first appeared.

The first of these historic transformations was the quantum revolution that shook physics during the first quarter of the present century and led to the rejection of many of the dominant ideas of Western thought, such as the rigidly determined world subscribed to by virtually all philosophers in the West, and the concept of a permanent, self-identical, not-further-analyzable substance. The second great transformation came when no traditional cultural identity was able to survive the rub of radically different racial, ethnic, linguistic, and cultural systems brought to the "new world" by the immigrants whose descendants form the overwhelming bulk of the population. A nation had emerged out of a spontaneously self-chosen population, initially from Europe but eventually from every part of the planet. During the two centuries following Jamestown and Plymouth Rock, inter-cultural communication became a law of life. The vast problems of settling a continent forced a polyglot population to turn its back upon all European models of civilization and to place the emphasis upon the original experience which individuals here were sharing with one another in everyday life. As Dewey later eulogized this radical departure from ancestral ways, "of all affairs communication is the most wonderful. That the fruit of communication should be participation, sharing, is a wonder by the side of which transubstantiation pales."[41]

The third and final factor is that many of the central ideas of the "Classic American Philosophers" had been anticipated in philosophers whose contributions might still be neglected and even forgotten except for the role they came to play in American process thought: Samuel Alexander's and C. Lloyd Morgan's "emergent evolution," Henri Bergson's classic view of the opposition between perception and conception, Étienne Boutroux's compatibility between causality and chance, Charles Darwin's famous repudiation of fixed species, Gustav Fechner's self-surpassable deity (dismissing the idea subscribed to throughout the European tradition that deity cannot change), C. Judson Herrick's aphorism that "making novelties seems to be nature's chief industry," Jules Lequier's equally provocative notion that "Thou hast created me creator of myself," and even more novel discoveries by David Hume, Sigmund Freud, Karl Marx, and Friedrich Nietzsche. Though none of these germinal thinkers was yet thinking of his work as "process philosophy," the term now everywhere in vogue, all were feeling out a world where creativity is an ultimate notion.

Like the other two process philosophies, which made their appearance in northern India and in Heraclitus's Greece, process thinking in its American mode constitutes a deep revolutionary challenge to the dominant ideas in which most inhabitants of this continent are reared. Like the other two philosophies, its central point is the tension between what is concrete, spontaneous, immediate, original, evanescent, and free in human experience, as Peirce puts it,[42] and the almost irresistible pressure of every established order to force human experience into the linguistic and institutional system already in place. The upsurges that shake the settled structures of individual and social existence bear witness to a deeper-than-conventional presencing of life. "The history of thought," Whitehead writes, "is a tragic mixture of vibrant disclosure and of deadening closure. The sense of penetration is lost in the certainty of completed knowledge. This dogmatism is the antichrist of learning."[43] Philosophers in the West have been, for the most part, unaware of the perils of abstraction. Heraclitus in Greece has been a voice in the wilderness.

Every effort to describe and conceptualize novel forms of awareness must be false to them, and in the last resort, humanly destructive. In the concrete experience of William James the point became a matter of life and death. "Yesterday," he writes, "was a crisis in my life. . . . Hitherto, when I have felt like taking a free initiative, like daring to act originally, without carefully waiting for contemplation of the external world to determine all for me, suicide seemed the most manly form to put my daring into; now, I will go a step further with my will, not only act with it, but believe as well; believe in my individual reality and creative power." Whitehead and Peirce made this point throughout their careers. "The willful adherence to a belief," Peirce writes, "and the arbitrary forcing it upon others must be given up." As Whitehead was to put the point later on, "Life refuses to be embalmed alive."[44]

Especially in its American mode, process philosophy is an effort to bring to the forefront of attention the outrage inflicted upon individualized experience when the contrived world of intellectual and institutional form is imposed upon the most precious of all natural resources—the incandescence and power of what is vivid in the momentary now. The formative events in the shaping of the American culture—the nation's territory tripling in less than two hundred years, its population multiplying fifty times, its resources growing with its sudden new sources of gold, railroads, and land—brought Americans face-to-face with the process in which a new society is born. "They know, because they have seen them made," Donald Cary Williams writes, "that societies are artificial combinations engineered by private citizens for their own ends."[45]

And so a philosophical revolution has been needed, to complete what was commenced in the political one, presupposing as a matter of course the goals already so nobly advanced—freedom from inequitable taxation, from control by an established church, from constraints on social improvement—and calling into question the more fundamental form of bondage that it is the business of philosophy to expose—the rule of unchosen abstractions over the original individualized experience of the momentary now. The ways of cultural imperialism are here exposed in their inexhaustible techniques of military, economic, political, linguistic, and, particularly, conceptual aggression. The age of a vast population deaf and dumb to the concreteness of their own experience can now recede into its European past. The idea has been germinating in American process thinking for a very long time that in the concreteness of things no man or woman is incapable of adding to the quality of life, whatever his or her racial or ethnic origin or background.

The new declaration of independence in this philosophical revolution was written by a transplanted Englishman who had been invited, after a distinguished career at Cambridge and London in mathematics, logic, and physics, to teach philosophy at Harvard, something he said at the time "he had always wanted to do," at the age of sixty-three. Addressing his Harvard colleagues about that institution's future, Whitehead carries the unfinished American revolution beyond the limits of the past. "For three centuries," he argues, "European learning has employed itself in a limited task. Scholars, in science and in literature, have been brilliantly successful. But they have finished that task—the possession of clear ideas, woven into compound structures, with the attributes of truth, or of beauty, or of moral elevation." "European learning," Whitehead continues, "was founded on the dictionary; and splendid dictionaries were produced. With the culmination of the dictionaries the epoch has ended." And further: "All the dictionaries of all the languages have failed to provide for the expression of the full human experience. . . . Experience does not occur in the clothing of verbal phrases."[46]

In this statement the Europeanization of the earth is called into question. A new awareness has dawned that conscious symbolic processes are not the primary vehicles of learning. A cognition-biased, definition-minded, concept-oriented, over-intellectualized European tradition stretching backward to the amazing Greeks is here effectively challenged. The world no longer exists to be known. The intellect is no longer the highest level of the soul. The attention has been shifted decisively away from a world of timeless truths, away from abstract systems of law, politics, and ecclesiastical form, over to a more fundamental way of experiencing the world. William James, Josiah Royce, Charles Peirce, John Dewey, Alfred North Whitehead, and their penetrating and judicious auditor Charles Hartshorne constitute this kind of fundamental break with the past, calling into question the dominant tendencies in Western philosophy—the search for ideas that no amount of empirical experience can ever falsify, the enthrallment with abstract reason over concreteness, the pursuit of some Archimedean point from which to move the world, the general denigration of the burgeoning present, and the entrapment in language which Wittgenstein found to be an almost irresistible matter of "bewitchment."[47]

In American process philosophy, creativity and freedom have found a home. Here, the happiness and value in the world are found in individuals: they alone enjoy and suffer the qualities of the fleeting instant; they alone give institutions whatever purposes they pursue. We, therefore, face the task, Whitehead writes, of providing for a universe that is without bounds, for a learning that is worldwide, and for an emotional life with springs lying below conventionalities. Civilizations are produced, according to Whitehead, "not so much by community of bare ideas as by community of feelings by which ideas are 'emotionalized' and become beliefs and motives." Such feelings, however, "are not in the first instance ours," Hartshorne argues, "but belong especially to creatures making up our bodies. The 'ocean of feelings,' each with some self-determination and some participation in previous feelings, is reality itself." These original qualities of the fleeting moment, furthermore, encounter their death-trap in the rule of convention: "A learned orthodoxy," Whitehead warns, "suppresses adventure," exhausting the creative springs of originality that are essential to civilization.[48]

The creativity and freedom found in American process philosophy cannot, however, be limited to each individual's experience; experience must be shared by all. Peirce frames the point in terms of logic and science: "Logicality," he writes, "requires that our interests shall not be limited, must not stop at our own fate, but must extend to all races of beings with whom we can come into immediate or mediate intellectual relations."[49] And Dewey's "reconstruction in philosophy"[50] directs attention away from what James called the "block universes" of European thought over to the shared individualized experience that in the very nature of the case is always beyond the reach of the sociological communities to which individuals belong.

Process philosophy in the American mode, therefore, turns Plato, Kant, and Hegel upside down, the main line of reality lying in no conception of anything in or beyond the world, reality being created from one moment to the next and inherited in its vast interrelatedness in memory and perception. The greatest single contribution to American process philosophy is Whitehead's revolutionary concept of prehension, one of the three concepts that constitute the core of "Whiteheadianism," the other two being creativity ("the universal of universals") and the actual entities of momentary occasions ("the really real things which in their collective unity compose the evolving universe, ever plunging into the creative advance").[51] Whitehead defines prehension in his famous statement that "the many become one and are increased by one."[52] Clarifying how the one experience in the fleeting moment synthesizes many past events, Whitehead's concept of prehension is an unprecedented theory of the way the world proceeds, only vague approximations being found in Bergson, Peirce, and Buddhism.[53] To make the concept possible, many careless habits of the Western tradition had to be overcome: its thingification of the world, its simple-minded submission to ordinary language and common-sense assumptions, its suspicion of new concepts, its confusion regarding the symmetrical nature of past and future, its prejudice with respect to an "inextended" mind and the dualisms naturally resulting therefrom, and its

queer propensity to look beyond the tops of the highest moun-
tains to something more fundamental than time and space and
history could ever contain. Reality is thus a new single event
related to and partly constituted by many events of the past.
Whitehead's world is self-creative, a balancing act between causality and change; creative change is an ultimate notion (as Peirce
writes at great length).

Whitehead's concept of prehension points to a form of causal
efficacy at work in the deeps of human personality, weaving new
textures of shared experience into the deepening and widening
community of life. It is here where men and women find their
reality and their truth. In these prehensions we coexist much
more than exist, influence others and are influenced by them,
carry forward in time the funded experience of the species, and
participate in the power that is acquired by caring, suffering, and
remembering compassionately what is happening and has happened in the life of the world. Long before we know what our
novel forms of togetherness portend, we are caught in their opa-
lescent grasp. There are many things in this mysterious world for
which we bear responsibility, but the forming of our conscious
minds is not one of them. Changes of mind are native growths
within a living organism, nurtured in the relational origination of
things rather than summoned into existence.[54] "To prehend," as
Hartshorne says, "is to sympathize with or participate in the feeling of others."[55]

In its most fully developed American form, process philosophy
speaks to us of a world that is always forming itself through the
creative communication of individual persons and things. Reality
is most unambiguously given, not at the verbal or institutional
levels of life, but in those novel forms of togetherness that find
their way into what is coming to be. Our own more or less intense
unverbalized experiences are the clearest and most indubitable
instances of what is actually real, a view that differs from the
ineffable experience found in European doctrines of mysticism
because here it is an empirical process present in everyday life, an
empirical process responsible for ordering the form of everything
that is coming to be. Deeper than the matters that separate individuals from one another, the common bond of our togetherness
is found at this experiential level, feeling the feelings of one an-

other and communicating out of an original experience in its non-verbal social growth. This is the same fundamental fact Guenther finds in Tibetan Buddhism—"its communicative unifying thrust."[56]

"The total concrete reality in a personal existence," Hartshorne says, "is new each moment," the latest in the career of an individual's life; it contains all there is to the unity of the self in whose personal character it occurs.[57] Because this concrete reality emerges as a subliminal upsurge coming out of the individual's relations with fellow-creatures and the organic wholeness of the world, it is the basis for our sense of being "members one of another," including the speechless world's fellow-creatures. ("The Buddhists had this in mind for many centuries," Hartshorne writes, "and in all branches of Buddhism; I think they have a precious lesson to teach Christians at this point."[58])

Process philosophy in the American mode is not as largely a historical miracle as it may seem. It is the positive contribution of a handful of Western civilization's most powerful minds, working over insights of a European legacy usually ignored and drawing out for the first time the implications of physical research conducted in places like CERN *(Conseil Européen pour la Recherche Nucléaire)* and the Fermi Institute at Batavia, Illinois. Even more crucially, a new historical matrix created for the first time on American shores had the possibility from the very outset of curing a human community of an affliction carried by civilized form and structure. More important by far than installations of high-tech research and discoveries in outer space, the chief discovery of the American community is the concreteness in the process of life. People here were simply unable to understand each other and solve their problems together as long as they allowed their minds to be shaped by their radically different ancestral linguistic and cultural backgrounds. Slowly but irresistibly, they came to accept the necessity of relating directly to one another's original experience in the new world. Their awareness of one another's "prehensions" became the occasion for influencing and being influenced by one another. They gradually stopped clinging to a world that had been projected for them by their ancestral traditions.

What Buddhism calls "relational origination," therefore, found in the American community its first cultural embodiment in the

West. And this cultural fact, rather than any grasp of the Buddha's teaching, is the source of Whitehead's embodiment of so many distinctive Buddhist perspectives.[59] In numerous explicit references to Buddhism he displays the most erroneous views.[60] Insights were forcing themselves to the surface that Whitehead was deliberately attempting to clarify, helping this community to think freely about the novel possibilities here and the futility of trying to transplant European cultures to American shores. Questions were being clarified here that had never been answered: What is it that men and women experience concretely, in relation to which everything else is abstract? What is experience as originally given, without the overlay of sensory form or the intrusion of conscious thought?[61] These are but two of the devastating new questions shaking existing institutions of law, government, philosophy, and religion.

Process philosophy in the three modes presented in this chapter represents the return of the native to the concreteness of the living moment, to the flow of quality within an organism acting as a whole, brain contemporary with the body, the complex amplifier that transforms vague feeling tones into the more vivid ranges of experience where men and women in the instantaneous present are memorably and vitally alive. Process thinking returns the individual from the high abstractions of conscious thought—following Aristotle's lead, Western philosophy simply could not see that the final, fully concrete units of reality are momentary, unit instances of becoming, rather than of being.[62] Thinking in the process mode, we are returned from the wholesale institutionalization of our lives, from the stereotyped ways we perceive the world through cultural clichés, and from the even more artificial data of the senses. Process philosophy is an effort to give individual men and women a foothold in a universe of which they are an organic part, a universe that enfolds their freedom with the implicate order of the whole.[63]

In its process form, philosophy has achieved a new relationship to human experience. Alphonse de Waelhens puts this point clearly in his recent survey of contemporary thought: "No longer an *explanation from afar* of the world and of consciousness, philosophy henceforth becomes *one* with this experience; not satisfied to shed light on man and his life, it aspires to *become this life,* now at the stage of complete self-awareness."[64] In America, process philosophy approaches this stage, the creation of a community of immigrants who are still exploring the vast continent of their experience on the crossroads of an interdependent world.

# 3. The Two Faces of Reason

*Greece was the mother of Europe; and it is to Greece that we must look
in order to find the origin of our modern ideas, transmitted to us, enriched
by the genius of Plato and Aristotle, shared in by all the races of western
Europe. The tale tells how a particular direction of reason emerges in a
race by the long preparation of antecedent epochs, how after its birth its
subject-matter gradually unfolds itself, how it attains its triumphs, how
its influence moulds the very springs of action of mankind. The moral of
the tale is the power of reason, its decisive influence on the life of
humanity.*

*Alfred North Whitehead,* Science and the Modern World

*The founding concepts of philosophy are primarily Greek, and it would
not be possible to philosophize, or to speak philosophically, outside this
medium. When Heidegger says, for example, that "for a long time, too
long, thought has been desiccated," like a fish out of water, the element
to which he wishes to return thought is still—already—the Greek element, the Greek thought of Being, the thought of Being whose irruption
or call produced Greece.*

*Jacques Derrida,* Writing and Difference

A creature that thinks as freely as we do cannot live by mere
impulsive drives or social coercion. Born without the required
competence for survival in the encompassing web of life, we form
our life-styles by taking thought, by maintaining a dialogue with
others, by inheriting reflections across many centuries and generations, from one civilization and culture-world to another.

In all but the most exceptional periods philosophical reflection finds itself locked into the task of keeping the linguistic and conceptual systems clear and relevant amid change. During times of volatile transformations in the conditions of life, however, philosophy may turn its critical eye upon the pretentious claims of ancestral order and tradition, "searching out," in Whitehead's words, "the unexpressed presuppositions which underlie the beliefs of every finite human intellect." During such times, people like Collingwood are suspected of provincialism in their arguments that some assumptions are so deeply rooted as to warrant being called the "absolute presuppositions of life"; people like Michel Foucault are so suspected for their views that a social paradigm controls the growth of knowledge in a culture and remains inaccessible to analysis until a new paradigm has emerged.[1]

Like the filter-plant monitoring the quality of the water in urban centers, philosophy has now gained new self-understanding enabling it to penetrate the supposedly fixed frameworks of the past. The hypnotic grip of parochial ways is being broken—by travel and migration, by millions of refugees annually on the move, by instantaneous communication between people living on all stages of human development, and by typhoons of information more powerful than the most vulgar ideological mind.

As a partial expression of the most radical transformation Western civilization has ever undergone, process philosophy for over a century has been struggling successfully against the natural inertia of thought, freeing the mind from the categories and conceptual systems that have given Western civilization its central core of ideas since it emerged out of the Mediterranean world from origins Hebraic-Christian and Greek.

With its new perspective that events and their relations are the ultimate form of concreteness, that immediate experience occurs in, to use Whitehead's phrase, "an ocean of feelings," that there is no going behind life's momentary nows to find anything more real, and that the world of becoming is, as Hartshorne says, "endlessly, inexhaustibly creative,"[2] process thinking has been imploding the intellectual houses in which generations upon generations in the West have endeavored to dwell. In arguing that simple sense data are the results of abstraction from the momentary now, and by insisting that persons and things are high-level abstractions from this unit of reality, process philosophy is confirmed by thinkers working technically in most areas of contemporary thought.[3] "The unity of the momentary experience is taken as primitive," Hartshorne writes; "there is no other unity from which it can be derived."[4] Inherited notions, therefore, of an ever-identical self that experiences everything that happens in a lifetime and of the Greek concept of a not-further-analyzable substance are no longer accepted as the mirror image of what is real. Substances fundamental for two millennia in mind, body, matter, spirit, and everything else considered real are now analyzed into momentary actualities, "throbbing moments," "pulsations of experience," in a process of perpetual becoming. What is completely real is process.

Cognition is not the whole story of knowing, as libraries of data on the split brain unambiguously show. For Hartshorne, "There is no independent faculty of cognition—feeling is the presupposed substratum." Because, however, as Whitehead argues, Descartes, Locke, and Hume utilized in their analysis of experience "those elements in their own experience which lie clear and distinct, fit for the exactitude of intellectual discourse," they launched modern philosophy in the West with an ancestral blindness from which it has only recently recovered in process thought, the blindness of not perceiving that the venture of knowing the world is based, not in ego-centered proprietary interests but in the resonance of humankind to the living world. Bergson puts it succinctly: "We think with only a small part of our resources; the intellect, so skillful in dealing with the inert, is awkward the moment it touches the living; *the intellect is characterized by a natural inability to comprehend life.*"[5] A new critique of the highly selective and artificial patterns of sense data and conceptual models is spreading in the contemporary world, generating a new kind of empiricism, which "runs in the veins of all of us as a common bond"; as Whitehead's biographer puts it, "We seek in empirical inquiry an approach that does not lock us into a partitioned mental stockroom."[6]

As persuasive as all of these developments are, though, process philosophy is not unchallenged in its struggle to displace the vision of Being and the cognitive bias inherited from the ancient

Greeks. The compulsive grip of Being lingers on in the effort of Martin Heidegger, for example, perhaps the most widely read of all contemporary philosophers, to return thinking to its Greek sources. The chief menace, indeed, that he sees assailing humanity is that the language of philosophy has fallen into a state of corruption such that the presence of Being has been concealed by an inability to ask the most fundamental question, an inability which has its source in a language that has wandered from the Greek fold. Heidegger's is the mightiest effort of the contemporary world to return to our spiritual-historical beginnings in Greece and reinstate the concept of Being to its central place in Western thought. Our age, he says, has forgotten what it means to be open to Being, and to accept our fundamental experience of the forgetfulness of Being.

Until the rise of process philosophy and its scientific counterpart in the quantum revolution in physics now nearly a century old, each rising generation in the West had been trained to interpret its experience in terms of the conceptual models inherited from the Greeks. As the British anthropologist Edmund Leach says, "European learning over the past two thousand years has rested on the assumption that all the essential categories of thought had already been devised by the fifth century B.C. The art of civilized living has consisted of slotting all new experiences into Ancient Greek categories—and then we knew how to cope."[7] These were the secure hitching posts to which perception in all of its ambiguities could be tied—at the expense, we now know, of the creativity, vividness, concreteness, and rich diversity in the individualized experience of all. With the revolution in modern high-energy physics, it has become possible on a broad scale for men and women to experience themselves in terms of events in the momentariness of life, with no dualisms of mind and body to sunder the unity and with no strict deterministic causal necessity to obscure the creativity of life.

## The Greek Accent on Form

Classical Greek thought is the world's most famous search for what is imperishable and unchangeable in the affairs of humankind. Nowhere has the concrete experience of individuals been placed so thoroughly under control by abstractions. No philosophers anywhere on earth have had such confidence in human thought's having a privileged path into the very heart of reality. In two of his greatest understatements, Whitehead writes about the Greeks that "they were unaware of the perils of abstractions" and that in actual fact "experience does not occur in the clothing of verbal phrases."[8]

European philosophy begins among the Greeks with their effort to discover the most universal of those vital truths by which human beings and the rest of nature unconsciously live. It is a quest for conceptual models as well proportioned and complete as the Greek temple, whose post-and-lintel harmony took three and a half centuries to reach perfection. Classical Greek thought looked forward to a community that would be governed by law, visible not to the senses but to the inner eye of reason. It was not concerned with what people empirically desired or sought to be; it attempted to discover what they would desire and seek if they were infinitely wiser than they were. Whether in poem, statue, drama, or music, the Greeks of the classical age were in search of the universal truth. Everywhere the most highly developed Greek mind was in dialogue with itself, looking for the rationally formulated meanings that point to the foundations of the world.

Flowing out of its sources in ancient Greece, Western civilization fell in love with abstractions, identifying reality with what can be thought. What can be grasped only by the highest faculty of reason is the substance of all that is real. Absolute and certain knowledge is the prime function of reason, and in all areas of a community's life—morality, politics, religion, and science—reason provides the truths that endure forever, truths that are applicable everywhere because they reveal what is deepest in the world. Conceptual thinking is therefore every community's highest occupation. Cognition discovers the forms in the nature of things with such certitude that no amount of empirical experience can ever call them into question. Hegel spoke this attachment to reason with utmost clarity for the first time in the modern world, believing as he did that "Reason is the substance of the Universe" and that "Reason embodied in the State is sovereign of the World."

The state thus has a rational essence superior to all individuals composing it. It is duty bound, therefore, to control art, education, economics, religion, and all cultural endeavors.

None of this was ever a merely academic or scholastic and purely philosophical concern. On the contrary, it was a matter of vital importance to a linguistically encapsulated culture seeking objective archetypes defining the horizon within which men and women would be expected to live. In the dominant tradition shaped by Plato, Aristotle, Descartes, Leibniz, Kant, and Hegel, the abstract universal is exalted over concrete particulars,[9] static being over becoming and change, strict causal necessity over freedom, conceptual knowledge over individualized experience, eternity over time, permanence and immutability over what Whitehead refers to as the "novel forms of togetherness" continually emerging out of the foundations of the world. Each of these features plays its distinctive dramatic role in the Aristotelian concept of God.

The philosophical conclusion that has been admired over the longest stretch of European thought is the concept of the Unmoved Mover, who has no environment to which to adapt and in whom all potentiality has been fully actualized—the supreme cause influenced by nothing in the world, who therefore knows nothing about the ambiguities of creatures who seek only to become more fully alive. To know such creatures would be a contradiction.[10] The most fully actualized and completely real is the most abstract. In this highest of all the forms of reality, we have the overarching model of the ego-centeredness deeply rooted in the dominant tradition of European thought. Aristotle's concept of deity is the most forceful illustration in the history of philosophy of the self-centered nonsocial self. Harry Wolfson has given us the picture:

*God, as an incorporeal being, is an immovable mover. Corporeal beings which are described as thinking have something external to themselves as the object of their thought; God has only himself as the object of His thought. Corporeal beings which are described as living possess a life which consists of nutrition, growth, and sensation; God's life consists only of the actuality of His own thought. Corporeal beings which are described as being pleased are pleased only at the satisfaction of a want; God's pleasure consists in the actuality of His own life. Corporeal beings which are described as being good have a goodness which is acquired by them from without; God's goodness consists in His contemplation of Himself.*[11]

With this model of perfection before them, it is not strange that self-interest and self-concern made the Christian exaltation of love an inconceivable and unattainable cultural goal.

This is the philosophical tradition by which, even today, leading figures "always know themselves to be overtaken," as Derrida puts it, the Greco-European conceptual tradition "now in process of taking over all of humanity."[12] With this Greek storehouse of the supersensible forms inherent in things, Europe has *never* ceased to view itself as the cultural center of the world. The classical European philosopher has been persuaded that apart from these traditional universally valid foundations there are no signposts giving direction to life, no security amid volatile change, no clues for educating the young, no way of solving ethical, political, and religious problems or avoiding ever more destructive wars.

All of this classical Greek accent on form with its obvious trade-off between a merely representational world and the surging creativity of original individualized experience might seem simply incredible, until the historical circumstances in which these ancient Greek categories were being generated twenty-five centuries ago have been considered. Thousands of modern scholars have traversed the territory covered by the ancient Greeks as they moved from a nonliterate culture stored in the memory of its members, the culture of events narrated by Homer and Hesiod, over to the culture found primarily in the written word. The conceptual metaphors and belief systems of the poets were telegraphing their exhaustion amid unavoidable and thoroughgoing social change. Until the fifth century B.C., the education of the ruling classes had been oral, poetic, mythic, and musical in nature.[13] As Wallace Matson says of the shift to the written word, it is marked by "a mutation of thought such as never happened independently anywhere else in the world: an intellectual Olympic leap compared to which every subsequent 'paradigm shift' is but a hop and a skip."[14] As Matson indicates in the title of his essay "From

Water to Atoms," the shift from the oral culture of Homer and Hesiod to the culture in which only a small minority could *read* was one of the fateful changes in the way of life, because it gave abstract ideas unprecedented power over the individualized experiences of everyday life.

It was this "intellectual Olympic leap" from the natural anthropomorphism of Hesiod and Homer over to the literate culture of universal abstract concepts that provided Western civilization with its intellectual models for the next two thousand years, models with which to control human behavior toward outcomes determined in advance, giving the small minority who had the leisure required for the pursuit of knowledge unprecedented power over the community at large. Amid the stress of volatile social change, Athens was moving to the place of eminence and esteem reserved for it in the West as the creator of a new language of abstract ideas, the discovery of the concept of the universal that would dominate the human mind for two thousand years, and a vision of Being which would regulate "and to a great extent dominate the vision of life."[15]

Social and intellectual changes of such magnitude resemble an earthquake in which "everything seems to sway."[16] The assumptive-form world of the past was being shaken and dislodged. Socrates was sentenced to drink the hemlock by a jury of five hundred Athenians, many of whom were deeply disturbed by the questions he was teaching the younger generation to ask. The date of Socrates' execution, 399 B.C., is branded on the minds of students everywhere. It was this event that persuaded Plato, then twenty-eight years of age, that Athens needed not another statesman but a school where justice could be taught and universal standards discovered from which the state could derive its authority to govern.

The number of poets, artists, and philosophers who stumbled and fell while Athens was making up its mind bears witness to the shaking of the institutional crust. Despite its reputation to the contrary, Athens had never been a model of tolerance toward opposing views. Lacking a clear method for composing differences and correcting beliefs, truth could be said to be on the side of the most widely accepted social power. A rising commercial class with a new monetary economy was developing connections in the wider Mediterranean world. Contact with foreign societies was bringing home for the first time the possibility that the community's conventions and laws were less firmly rooted than previously supposed in a divine ordering of things. Protagoras of Abdera was banished and his books burned in the market-place because, like other Sophists, he was pressing for novelty in political and religious affairs; he was not teaching his eager students to repeat what the rulers wanted them to be told. Anaxagoras, the great philosopher of the Periclean Age and one of the first to advance an atomic theory of reality, was indicted and sentenced to death for denying that the sun and the moon are divine (though Pericles, uncrowned king of Athens, who had been Anaxagoras's student, was able to secure his release). The great sculptor Phidias was arrested for sacrilege and died in prison.

Sophocles and, to even greater extent, Euripides were questioning the justice of the divine order of the world. The Athenian crowd rose to its feet in protest as Euripides had Melanippe question the very existence of Zeus and fling defiance at the old religious myths. In the same vein, Sophocles has Philoctetes say:

*The gods seem to take delight in turning back the wicked and*
*deceitful from the tomb,*
*And sending there all that is good and honest.*
*What can I think, how praise the ways of God,*
*When I find evil in the gods themselves?*[17]

The Greeks were not very far, culturally speaking, from "the death of God."

Such was the Olympic leap that, as Matson says, made every future paradigm shift "a mere hop and a skip": The Greeks were using abstractions to displace the Homeric gods. Universal ideas were being put forth as the models with which to control behavior. The problem of unbelief was present in such intensity that it could not continue to be solved by simple banishment, imprisonment, or execution. A long list of Greek thinkers were trying to shore up the ancestral order by placing abstractions at the zenith of life. The idea became the "whatness" of the thing; language became the custodian of Being. It was this Greek transmutation of human existence upon which Plato placed the finishing touches.

As William Wordsworth was to remark centuries later, in the face of the social ferment and revolution in the France of his day, the hopes of men and women were being abstracted out of their feelings, "to be fixed thenceforth forever in a purer element of the mind."[18]

His own elevation of abstractions to the role formerly played by religion led Hegel to greet the French Revolution with enthusiasm, although the Terror of 1793 caused him to moderate his view. The men of the revolution, Hegel writes, were the first to try to reorganize human living under the demands and specifications of thought. Hegel applauded the effort: "As long as the sun was in the firmament and the planets revolved around it, no one had ever seen man stand on his head, i.e. upon thought, and construct reality in accordance with it. Anaxagoras was the first to say that *nous* rules the world; but now man had come to recognize that thinking should govern spiritual activity. This was therefore a splendid dawn."[19]

From the time of the Olympic leap, Western civilization at the highest level became an adventure in knowing. Without any feedback from the concrete experience of particular men and women, human reason endeavored to provide principles that would give intelligible order to life, linking it to some goal or good for which more or less exact rational justifications have been drawn. A volatile civilization was committed to seeking stability and direction in the forms of thought, where knowledge would grow by transcending the individual moment, fabricating a world of abstractions in which the love and compassion and the suffering of particular people would have no room.

## The Return to Experience

Looking down the long vista of European philosophy beginning with the great intellects of the classical Greeks, we can see the eventual encounter of classical Western thought with its own gravediggers: nihilism, logical positivism, the Vienna Circle, phenomenology, existentialism, and other technical ways of saying that there is no essential form of the world in which the human mind can find itself at home. Each one following upon the dilemmas of the other, all have unwittingly collaborated in bringing to an as-yet-undeclared state of bankruptcy the ancient effort of the Greeks to balance the world upon thought.

The hegemony of Europe in the philosophical chambers of the world has now come to an end. Legacies as ancient and even older than the West, particularly those from India, China, and Tibet, are being heard in the most consecrated centers of Western thought. Fixed conclusions are being reopened in the light of new points of view. Questions are being asked all over again: How is reality experienced and known? What are the limits of language? What is meant by personal identity? And at least one conclusion is being drawn out of these philosophical encounters with the non-Western world: The hope is being abandoned that human experience in all of its individualized vividness and concreteness can be subsumed under the abstract universal without alienating the human creature from life. Experience—which for Charles Peirce "is our only teacher"—is richer and more fascinating with vivid quality and creativity than any abstract overlay of sense data, language, and cultural form. As Hartshorne says, "Experience is of bodily processes, whatever other data there may be."[20]

As early as the fourteenth century a succession of courageous and brilliant men—Roger Bacon, Duns Scotus, and William of Ockham among them—commenced placing the claims of abstract theoretical constructs in check, rejecting demonstrations of the existence of God, shifting the spotlight of attention to human experience instead of simply looking beyond it, and suggesting that the only certainty human beings have any basis for expecting is to be found in experience itself. "Everything is absolute," as Ockham remarks; except in our thoughts, only individuals exist. Six centuries ago the idea was beginning to take hold that the world could have been other than it is and that our forms of understanding do not lead to necessary supersensible forms inherent in the nature of things. Slowly the opinion was taking root that traditional doctrines and conceptual systems were not the only way a sane person might think about the world.

Despite the continuing dominance in some philosophical circles of what Robert Bellah calls the "Greek cognitive bias,"[21] it is now possible to see that a second face of reason is struggling to become more fully born, rejecting the enthrallment with abstractness over concreteness, static perfection over creative change, predictability over freedom, and the entrapment in language that has been so extreme that Wittgenstein could say "outside language you cannot breathe, you must always turn back."[22] This second face of reason is distinguished by a great renunciation. The search has been given up for some Archimedean point from which to move the world. Reason will now operate within the limits of experience, clarifying the range, vividness, wholeness, and superior richness of that experience, in order to foster, as Whitehead says, "the art of life."[23]

The first systematic struggle to check or reverse the Western tendency to go willingly into the concentration camp of what can be defined and formulated is associated with the work of Galileo (1564–1642), Francis Bacon (1561–1626), and Isaac Newton (1642–1727), all, according to Whitehead, "prophets of the historical revolt which deserted the method of unrelieved rationalism." "The way in which the persecution of Galileo has been remembered," Whitehead believes, "is a tribute to the quiet commencement of the most intimate change in outlook which the human race had yet encountered. Since a babe was born in a manger, it may be doubted whether so great a thing has happened with so little stir."[24] The cultures of Europe were coming alive with scientific investigations that drove a fissure into the firmly rooted habit of modeling everything in the mirror of abstract conceptual form. Against formidable odds, the emphasis in knowing was shifting away from conceptual systems, however valid within their chosen sphere, over to the self-corrective inquiry that has distinguished science from other cultural activities ever since.

The foundations of linguistic and cultural systems, however, change as slowly as the weathering of rock. Following its brilliant seventeenth-century beginnings, the West's "cultures of belief" continued to hold the upper hand, controlling scientific investigations under the demands of the established order of life. It is no accident that the problems with which Newton's *Principia* is preoccupied "are those whose solution was required before Britain could become a great imperial power and create the industrial revolution, problems such as the measurement of time, calculation of longitude and the tides, improvement of artillery, rational design of objects such as ships moving through a resisting medium, and the behavior of gases and liquids flowing through pipes."[25]

And the whole world remembers that as late as the twentieth century science presented the spectacle for several decades of different biologies for East and West.[26] The pressures of nationalism have, in fact, treated science as an indentured servant, restricting free and open inquiry to the most efficient weapons of destruction. Bound in its vast unanticipated power, science has been harnessed to the task of finding new concepts to live by, concepts with which to suppress protests against the established order of life. (The modern fate of this most intimate change in outlook which the human race has yet encountered will be discussed at length in chapter 6.)

Immanuel Kant is a major figure in the history of the rise of the second face of reason in the West—reason within the limits of experience—because of the way he dulled the force of the skepticism of David Hume. Hume had analyzed human impressions of the world and failed to find the very categories long presupposed for a meaningful life: God, freedom, causality, selfhood, and immortality. Remarkably analytic and pragmatic in his bent of mind, Hume was "keenly attuned to the passing concreteness of experience, prior to all forms and all conclusions, prior to the dominant cognitive paradigms of abstract reason."[27] He was more sensitive than his fellow-creatures to the socially pressurized cabin of cultural assumptions that prevent an individual from probing life's holiest depths. For Kant, on the other hand, the proper role of the mind was to provide the law and order required for living in an otherwise chaotic sensory and experiential world. Like other great defenders of the Greek legacy, Kant was unable to think from the feeling side of experience. He *thought* first. And the original freedom and spontaneity of what Peirce would call "First" had already flown.[28]

For Kant, not only those conceptions that turned up missing in Hume's analysis, but every category of intellectual value fails to appear when we analyze our empirical impressions in their immediate quality and flow. For Kant, the essential categories are rooted, not in the concreteness of our individualized experience, but in the structure of the human mind, the source of order and meaning for humankind. Whatever knowledge we have is a human artifact mediating between the structure of the mind and the way the world is in itself, beyond the reach of our probing. Reality is not directly accessible to us through our direct encounter with life. Beyond the phenomena ordered by the mind lies the supersensible sphere from which the raw material of knowledge comes. Freedom, for example, is a transcendental idea that contains nothing of the immediate qualities of our individualized experience. Freedom is a property of the transcendental ego, the pure self whose nature and destiny lies in the noumenal world outside and beyond what is directly felt. After the fashion of his Protestant background, Kant characterizes the human creature as a member of a kingdom beyond the realms of nature, confined to the representational world in order to make room for something called "faith."

Kant's powerful influence upon the ethical, epistemological, metaphysical, and religious interests of the modern world serves to remind us of the almost irresistible commitment of Western civilization to the cognitive bias of inherited systems of belief. In Kant the struggle continues at an even more anxious pace for the discovery of principles of authority with which to control behavior. The search is intensified for concepts that no amount of empirical experience can ever call in question.

The story of Western philosophy for much of the past four centuries has been a growing realization that the individual in the experiences of everyday life exists in a state of unrelieved fundamental estrangement. Kant raised this source of anxiety and suffering to new levels by not only presupposing but also offering new arguments to explain this basic alienation. As Kant sees the problem, pure individualized experience in its original vividness and intensity is lost at the outset in the process of discovering the essential features of the world. As George Schrader says, "The possibility of human knowledge in Kant presupposes the alienation of man from himself and the world, and the development of knowledge only accentuates the alienation."[29]

The long struggle to find a more creative role for abstractions appears in Hegel to have won, as the second face of reason seems to emerge to dominance over the Greek accent on form. Closer examination, however, shows that the victory has been achieved by one of the oldest maneuvers in the arsenal of established conceptual systems. A new *definition* of experience appears on the central European stage. One of Europe's most brilliant minds is still speaking with a dictionary at his back. His is still a philosophy of consciousness; our thought grasps experience in its full nature. He is not interested in the concrete individualized experience of everyday life. Experience is a metaphysical notion, not the feeling of the moment as it passes. Hegel's is another in the long line of efforts in the West to balance the world upon thought.

Hegel, who plays an important role in the emergence of what I have called the second face of reason partly because of the way his most famous student, Karl Marx, is even now changing huge portions of the world and partly because of his own struggle to overcome the fragmentation and alienation of life in the modern world, accepts the fact that men and women have lost the ability to identify with their own socio-linguistic systems and that their lives constitute a long and unaccountable experience of estrangement. He accepts the fact that people no longer feel at home in the world, a problem aggravated by the philosophy of Descartes; he even considers this estrangement an emergency in the viability of Western civilization. The thrust of Hegel's entire philosophical system is to demonstrate that, given the proper forms of understanding, "the experiences of the world of culture can cause spirit to 'return into itself' and define itself in increasingly adequate terms, until the pure 'I,' the self-thinking concept, becomes its own explicit object." The self-differentiating "I" is for Hegel the soul of the world. "The universality of the 'I' enables it to abstract from everything, even from its own life."[30]

Like all major philosophers after Descartes, Hegel propounds a higher unity in which the dualism of the *cogito* and the world can be overcome. His older contemporary Fichte, for example, beginning with the European persuasion that everything is abstract except absolute being and the absolute self, sought to bridge the dualism by absorbing everything into the self: "Since there is no way of reconciling the not-self with the self, let there be no not-self at all." Hegel's younger contemporary Schelling also speaks of a higher unity, "the holy abyss from which everything emerges and into which everything returns."[31] Traveling the highways of the world with Hegel, though, we should discover our pure self-thinking "I" and be restored from our estrangement by an awareness of the Absolute in us. What Hegel has in mind with the term "experience" is the parousia of the Absolute; experience is the presence of Being. As Heidegger says of Hegel, "Experience is the dialogue between natural consciousness and absolute knowledge. Natural consciousness is the *Zeitgeist*, the Spirit as it exists historically at any given time. But that spirit is not an ideology. As subjectness, it is the reality of the real."[32]

Hegel therefore illustrates the underlying theme of Western civilization—the effort to turn people away from the concreteness of life and view themselves as modeled in the mirror of abstractions. He is the natural progeny of the Greek faith in the accessibility of reality to reason. Kant left reality hidden behind abstractions. Hegel went to the opposite extreme. In Hegel, "reality is entirely open," Hartshorne writes, "open and accessible to us through its appearances, almost as though *we* were God."[33] But abstract structures continue to conceal the concrete feelings of everyday life.

One of the great efforts to penetrate the cultural membrane of abstractions and to think from the feeling side of experience is associated with the work of Karl Marx, easily Hegel's most famous student, who argues that "to Hegel the life-process of the human brain, i.e., the process of thinking, which, under the name of 'the Idea,' he even transforms into an independent subject, is the demiurgos of the real world, and the real world is only the external, phenomenal form of 'the Idea.' "[34]

It is Marx's unforgettable thought—not highly advertised in the West—that men and women have to fight against the alienation that is rooted not in the way the intellect naturally functions, as with Kant, nor in the Absolute that "pipes the tune" to which Hegel was dancing,[35] but in the way human labor is distorted in its creativity by an abstract world of social structures and ideas. For Marx, men and women have to struggle against their own tendencies to cling to theories and things that have been substituted for head and heart (a perception anticipated in Buddhism two millenia before); they have to free themselves from linguistic and conceptual systems that reflect the interests of a social class. The major thrust of Marx, indeed, is to return humankind from overarching cultural superstructures into the dynamic matrix of world-transforming human labor. According to Marx, men and women are acting and living authentically, that is to say in accord with their real nature, when they live and act to take all the abstract formulations back into the creative concreteness of everyday life: "The actual individual man must take the abstract citizen back into himself and, as an individual man in his empirical life, in his individual work and relationships, become a species-being; man must recognize his own forces as social forces, organize them and thus no longer separate social forces from himself in the form of political forces. Only when this has been achieved will human emancipation be completed."[36]

The locus of the creativity that transforms the world, according to Marx, is to be found in the practical-critical activity of human labor. It is a creativity characterizing the individual's interchange with fellow-creatures as well, and nothing could be more natural than that this creativity would find in the established order of large-scale social institutions an initial resolve to keep everything as it presently is (Buddhism shares Marx's suspicion of all large-scale institutions as rooted in proprietary compulsive attachments). At all periods in history the activity of human labor has been faced with various forms of obstruction, in struggling with which a wealth of new talents and capabilities have emerged.

It is *not* Marx's view, as has been so widely believed, that a self-moving historical process will bring forth its own antidote to these human problems. What is possibly distinctive of Marx's thought, indeed, is that the predisposition of an entire culture-world—the collective weight of traditions—is seen as too powerful for individuals working in isolation. For Marx, only an entire social class can be expected to abolish alienation by tearing up its roots. As Lucien Goldman states, "When men are able to enact their thinking so as to turn history on its hinges, then the identity appears for which Western philosophy has been seeking, the identity of thought and thing, embodied in a circumstance-changing transformation of the world."[37] A more grandiose and pretentious statement of the deepest assumptions of what Derrida calls "the primarily Greek concept of philosophy" has probably never been written. Unfortunately, in spite of Marx's insight into causes of alienation, he is one of the greatest exemplars of the Western fascination with a conceptual system; he is, as Tawney once remarked, "the last of the schoolmen."

Of the two most brilliant adversaries of Hegel's philosophy—Marx and Søren Kierkegaard—the latter is the more aware of the tendency in Western thought to disregard the concrete individualized experiences of everyday life. Kierkegaard is the major source of what has been called the "Existentialist Revolt" in modern thought. "The age," for Kierkegaard, "has forgotten what it means to exist, and what inwardness is. It has lost faith in the truth that inwardness makes the apparently scanty content richer. The whole concept of objectivity which has been made into our salvation is merely the food of sickness. . . . Our age has forsaken the individuals in order to take refuge in the collective idea. . . . One learns to know in passing what faith is, and so that is known. Another day astronomy is brought up, and so we gad our way through all the sciences and all the spheres, without ever living," without meeting the existential tasks face to face.[38]

European thought has had other rebels against the overintellectualization of life—Pascal, Rousseau, and the thirteenth-century Francis of Assisi are examples. But Kierkegaard was the first to fashion a veritable Western access road into Buddhism.[39] He is one of the leading influences, therefore, in the philosophical trajectory out of the almost inaccessible rarified atmosphere of abstract thought into the concrete individualized passing moments of everyday life. His is one of the most powerful efforts to free men and women from the tendency to rely upon a small intellectual elite from whom they have learned to think about the world as though they were not in it as an organic part.

The first successful step in this direction, as I have said, came with the brilliant seventeenth-century beginnings of modern science. It was almost predictable that philosophers sooner or later would reject prescientific speculative metaphysics and explore the possibilities for developing a new authoritative philosophical language based on the findings of science. This effort to transmute science into modes of understanding of special interest to academic philosophers emerged at the end of World War I, probably as a response to the murderous slaughter of an entire generation at places like Château-Thierry and Verdun, followed by cynical efforts at Versailles to keep traditional belief systems and existing social institutions intact.

Expressing itself in many forms variously called logical empiricism, logical positivism, and philosophies of language, these housecleaning overtures often attempted to reduce the language of science to the observations and methods out of which it had been built. "Science is a system based on direct experience," Rudolf Carnap says, "and it is controlled by experimental verification."[40] More and more, all versions of these modern analytical movements became absorbed in questions of methodology. Motivated at the outset by the need to free human understanding from its moorings in traditional abstract systems, these movements have recast philosophy in the light of its epistemological concern. Knowing has been and must remain the controlling pursuit of all thought that understands itself. According to Richard Rorty, the "mainstream philosopher" must speak in the accents of epistemology: "Now that such-and-such a line of inquiry has had such a stunning success, let us reshape all inquiry, and all of culture, on its model, thereby permitting objectivity and rationality to prevail in areas previously obscured by convention, superstition, and the lack of a proper epistemological understanding of man's ability accurately to represent nature."[41] In this way analytical philosophy, which Rorty sees as having absorbed all truly *modern* philosophy, has turned away from what we have been calling "the individualized experiences of everyday life," what Peirce was in the habit of thinking of as the aesthetic foundations of logic, ethics, and all other areas of human thinking.

Notwithstanding this tendency of the analytical movement to increase human bondage to what can and cannot be said, some of its members continue to include in their concept of philosophy more than its critical efforts to find a common world on the intellectual level of life. Some, like Ed Garlan, have become interested in the distinctive Buddhist focus on the feeling level of experience. Trained at Columbia University as an analytical philosopher, Garlan accepted a Fulbright appointment at the University of Mandalay and spent many weekends at the International Institute for Advanced Buddhistic Studies in Rangoon. He saw more than a slight resemblance between Wittgenstein and the analytical method of the historical Buddha. Garlan believes that Wittgenstein, whose revolutionary outlook has yet to be assimilated in the West, has this in common with the Buddha, that in both there is the same meticulous handling of small items of consciousness, in themselves often of no apparent significance, until as a final cumulative impact of the analysis one is struck silent, instead of running out on all sides in fragments of discursive thought. The analysis of the Buddha, Garlan sees, is broader in scope, having as its aim a general program for living and an analysis not only of language but of life.

It should be pointed out that the trajectory I have been tracing is confirmed by Whitehead in a remark about Bergson. "On the whole," Whitehead writes, "the history of philosophy supports Bergson's charge that the human intellect tends to ignore the fluency, and to analyze the world in terms of static categories."[42] Having discussed Bergson in two previous books, I will merely remind readers of his historic role in returning men and women from the wasteland of abstractions into the joy and creativity of life's rich qualitative flow. "Let us expand our thought," he says; "let us strain our understanding; break, if need be, all our frameworks, but let us not claim to shrink reality to the measure of our ideas."[43] The brain, Bergson declares, is a reducing-valve, its conceptual productions impoverishing the affirmation of worth that is life itself.

The emergence of phenomenology around two German universities, Heidelberg and Freiburg, particularly in the wake of World War I, is part of "the return to experience" that seeks to awaken men and women from their socially induced predisposition to move like homing pigeons toward ideas, ideologies, historic doctrines, and creeds, turning their backs upon the qualitative fullness of their own experience. A phenomenologist himself and a student of Edmund Husserl, Marvin Farber sees what is new in Western philosophy as "the effort to account for the 'origin' of the various structures of ordered experience and knowledge." Furthermore, "if phenomenology is taken to mean the same as 'descriptive philosophy of experience,'" Farber continues, "it is necessary to acknowledge the fact that in Peirce, James, Dewey, Ducasse, and C. I. Lewis it has had an independent American history, quite apart from the recent influence of Husserl."[44] Phenomenology, both German and American, shares with all process thought an explicit rejection of the two concepts around which so much of Western philosophy has revolved—the Greek-originated concepts of substance and being.

Both phenomenology and process thought, as discussed in the preceding chapter, are philosophies of experience, devoted to probing more deeply into the individualized forms of awareness of particular people. This is what distinguishes these philosophies from that of the enchanting Martin Heidegger, whose writings are more abundant and more widely read than those of any philosopher in the last hundred years. Heidegger is *not* interested in probing immediate experience in all its diversity, richness, and creativity. He is looking to see what makes experience possible; he is looking for something that is never discerned by the uncritical observer, something operating behind our backs yet inseparable from being spoken in language: "For Heidegger as for Hegel, there is no difference between the nature of being and speech about being; being is inseparable from being-spoken in language; and to speak of being is to tell what it is."[45]

Hanging upon every word Heidegger has spoken about Nietzsche, Heraclitus, Hegel, and Kant (yet not about what these thinkers said, but about what they would have said had they seen the implications Heidegger finds in their writing), a broad community of readers with unsated appetite await further publications of his prodigious labors. Caught in their own onesidedness and homelessness, they read Heidegger out of their disquieting hope that when he speaks about Being, and the Being of beings, a new meaning may come to them from the very beginnings of our spiritual historical existence in ancient Greece. This, after all, is what Heidegger intends. Throughout his writings he is using Plato, Aristotle, Descartes, and other major figures in the Western intellectual world to clarify his own probing into what these thinkers left unthought, what they may have dimly seen but shrank back from saying. Heidegger is looking for fresh opportunities for perceiving what is embedded in human life as its ultimate unsayable meaning. What he is asking in all of his nostalgia is that we find our way back into a world that is "worlding" on its own, where Being is forever presencing itself in ways we are incapable of discerning.

Alfred Hofstadter summarizes Heidegger's philosophy as an effort

> *to exist as a human being in an authentic relationship as mortal to other mortals, to earth and sky, to the divinities present or absent, to things and plants and animals; it*

*means, to let each of these be—to let it presence in openness,*
*in the full appropriateness of its nature—and to hold oneself*
*open to its being, recognizing it and responding to it appro-*
*priately in one's own being, the way in which one oneself*
*goes on, lives; and then, perhaps, in this ongoing life one may*
*hear the call of the language that speaks of the being of all*
*these beings and respond to it in a mortal language that*
*speaks of what it hears. To understand how man may think*
*in this way, recalling to mind the being that has, according*
*to Heidegger, long been concealed in oblivion, one must*
*understand the nature of the language by which thinking is*
*able to say what it thinks. The speech of genuine thinking*
*bids all that is to come—world and things, earth and sky,*
*divinities and mortals—to come, gathering into the simple*
*onefold of their intimate belonging together.*[46]

One can see why Hartshorne calls Heidegger "that mystic without an ethics." It is, however, as Robert Magliola says, a logocentric mysticism in the severest form, caught in the house of language, or in Heidegger's words, "the lighting-concealing advent of
being itself."[47] There is nothing we can do to participate, except
open ourselves to Being's unpredictable presencing, as it comes
into our lives in its finished-somewhere-somehow form.

The great distance European philosophy must travel before it
can free itself from its own reifications has not been appreciably
shortened by Heidegger's labors. Indeed, in its long history out of
Greek sources, Western philosophy has seldom placed greater
obstacles before human experience than those presented by
Heidegger's thought. Despite its promise of offering something
new from one volume to the next, his philosophy leaves us with
the traditional Greek models. If he intended to produce insights
into the second face of reason—reason within the limits of experience in its true vastness—his nostalgic intention remains as
hidden as the Being in the center of his system.

That the world is other than the way it appears in conceptual
thinking is something every emotionally stable person knows—
unless some ulterior motive is involved. Indeed, it is obvious
even to the emotionally disturbed that no one is ever fully at

home in a world of conceptual structure. No one seriously doubts, moreover, that we are the species which comes with the distinguishing mark of not knowing how to live, that we are overtaken from time to time by massive global transformations, and that we are presently caught between the backworldsmen whose "other world" has become a cruel dehumanized "celestial naught" and the small armies of contemporary philosophers trying valiantly to clarify our capacity for thinking and acting our way to the preanalytic awareness in which creatures like ourselves unconsciously live.

Western philosophy in its preoccupation with the dictionary has been unable to think from the feeling side of experience. Launched by the precocious Greeks down the long thoroughfare to its eventual encounter with nihilism, alienation, anxiety, fragmentation, violence, and suffering over the loss of a sense of identity, the dominant philosophies of the West have lacked a clear idea of experience as self-active, as creatively bringing along its own past into the vast interrelatedness of the living world. Persuaded that, according to Heidegger, "abstract thought is the highest form of existence, and that life should be an experiment of knowers," they "saw too little," Hartshorne writes, "the superior richness of the concrete and particular."[48] The Greeks and their Western progeny remained enthralled with the theoretical component in experience, assuming its basic one-to-one complementarity with reality itself. And so they handed down to the contemporary world their prejudice against experience as individualized, against momentary events and processes as the concrete level of reality, and against the continuing emergence of novel forms of togetherness. All creativity was allocated to God.

Process philosophy, critic of the abstractions and assumptions of what Edith Hamilton eulogized as the "Greek Way," constitutes the latest chapter in the history of Western thought. It is an adventure in penetrating ever deeper into the nature of things, holding its own persuasions forever under suspicion in the light of the circumstances to which they are addressed. For process philosophers, logic and mathematics are methods of inquiry, rather than clear and distinct statements of the limits of intelligibility. Whitehead, for example, baffled his auditors by looking forward to a future state of knowledge when the ambiguities of ordinary language and scientific explanation will have been over-come through a wider use of symbolic logic, his "first love."[49] For Whitehead, symbolic logic would greatly extend our ability to explore the concrete fullness of existence, enabling future genera-tions to deal effectively with an unlimited number of "real vari-ables" and thus cope with complexity such as no previous age has ever imagined. "Many mathematicians and scientific linguists," on the other hand, "must have had the experience," Benjamin Whorf writes, "of 'seeing,' in one fugitive flash, a whole vast sys-tem of relationships never before suspected of forming a unity. The harmony and scientific beauty in the whole vast system momentarily overwhelms one in a flood of aesthetic delight."[50]

What we are discovering in the process philosophies now enjoying the attention of a growing portion of the scholarly world is a new appreciation of the uses of reason and a deeper grasp of what it means to understand. I have traced the trajectory of Euro-pean thought in which hundreds of splendid minds, most of whom remain anonymous, gave their last full measure of devo-tion to experience a universe that, as Peirce says, "has emergence and novelty built into the very core of its being."[51] Some of these philosophers lost their own emotional health in the struggle against a convention-bound, institution-centered, ego-dominated, encapsulated culture. For four years, while his youthful mind was wrenching itself free from fixed traditions, Hume lived on the borderline of mental and emotional breakdown. His psychoso-matic troubles and the liver tumor or ulcerative colitis with which in all probability he died are known to be aggravated, to say the least, by the tensions attending emotional crises of this kind. Others, like Nietzsche, lost their lives in forms of insanity. Spinoza and Peirce were excommunicated and driven into retire-ment.[52] Peirce speaks for perhaps hundreds of thousands over the centuries: "Wherever you are, let it be known that you seriously hold a tabooed belief, and you may be perfectly sure of being treated with a cruelty no less brutal but more refined than hunt-ing you like a wolf."[53]

Our most responsible probes marking progress toward the second face of reason are part of repeated arduous flights toward the empirical, seeking to reconceive and more adequately express the fundamental essencelessness of things. They are forms of awareness whose prime function is to free individuals from self-centered and class- and culture-encapsulated structures designed to direct life toward goals determined in advance. They are designed to moderate the suffering that has attended the rule of conscious and unconscious compulsive drives. Hartshorne puts it this way: "Understanding must justify itself by enriching the present; something is wrong if understanding robs us of peace in the present, only so that we may, given luck, prolong our anxious existence into old age."[54]

Our trajectory out of the "Greek Way," therefore, has landed us in the more generous aesthetic richness of the "Buddhist Way," where all growth in awareness is marked by the ability to attend to more of the qualities of the passing moment, "to set free," in Ramanan's phrase, "the sense of the real from its moorings in abstractions." It is what Whitehead means in his famous statement that "the function of reason is to promote the art of life."[55] My next chapter shows how the most famous philosopher in the long Buddhist tradition defends what Kierkegaard called "the point of view."

# 4. Nāgārjuna

*Nāgārjuna did not want to establish any fixed dogma; he rather aimed at wiping out all views. This "theory of no-theory" was already found in the scriptures of early Buddhism. In order to understand his philosophy certain assumptions of the commentators and many modern students regarding the interpretation of his statements should be set aside. He cuts away the verbiage of speculative philosophy, and annuls the meaningless concepts and propositions. There is nothing inconsistent with the legend that he dabbled in science.*

Hajime Nakamura, Indian Buddhism

It is the almost unanimous decision of major Buddhist scholars working with the legacy in all of its forms that Nāgārjuna is the greatest authority for showing why the teachings of the historical Buddha have never become imprisoned in words, sacred scripture, ecclesiastical ritual, and conceptual system. Nāgārjuna's contemporary significance is indicated by Leroy Finch: "There are few philosophers who are more relevant to the situation today. At a time when the various metaphysical systems of the Western world are thrown into doubt and are beginning to cancel each other out, the vast and fearless all-devouring scepticism of Nāgārjuna comes like a breath of fresh air into Western philosophy. He stands for pursuing the path of impermanence and self-correction to the end where it culminates in liberation and complete openness, and not (as suggested by Nietzsche) in fear, panic and chaos."[1]

Two of the central features of all contemporary process thinking are clearly expressed in this most controversial of all Buddhist philosophers: the concepts of reality as a social process and of the creativity, spontaneity, momentariness, and unrepeatability of the experiences of everyday life. These two features, which constitute the uniqueness of the historical Buddha's teaching, are stated distinctly and aggressively in everything Nāgārjuna wrote. It was out of such a process view—the first one to appear on the planet—that Buddhism formulated its original understanding of suffering and its cure, and its compassion for other lives. Wherever Buddhism has managed to speak of and for itself, its focus has been upon the individualized momentary experience as it flows, and not upon the theoretical models and logical constructions in which Western philosophy from its ancient origins among the Greeks has been almost stubbornly engrossed. One of the keys to understanding Buddhism in its original forms, as well as in its most fully developed philosophical elaborations, is that even in its negations, such as the nonself *(anātman)*, it is *affirming* the process nature of the world. Buddhism has always been committed to breaking the linguistic and cultural shell in which people have been reared, enabling them to become more vividly aware as individuals of their dialogue with the living world. Nāgārjuna's thinking, therefore, is not "a dialectics of negation," as Alfonso Verdu has recently charged.[2] His dialectic in its deepest sense is an emphasis upon reality as a social process that *no* sociological community has ever understood. He indeed devotes much of his *Mūlamadhyamakakārikā* to explaining that the major concepts of *śūnyatā* and *pratītya-samutpāda* are not rejections of the world.[3]

What needs to be balanced in understanding Nāgārjuna is that the passing moments, while the sources of all motion through their creative synthesis of past and present, are part of the interrelatedness of existence *(śūnyatā)*, whose all-embracing togetherness excludes any self-generating, self-maintaining nature existing by reason of itself. As Vicente Fatone puts it in quoting an early Buddhist manuscript, "In *śūnyatā* there is no destruction."[4] There is only the process of what Whitehead calls "the becoming of experience,"[5] each being overtaken and increased by a new experience, as creative moments *(dharmas)* "prehending" the past into the novel togetherness of the present.

Nāgārjuna, whose name conjures up apparently endless argumentation among contemporary Buddhist philosophers and philologists, even as it has among their counterparts of the past eighteen hundred years, was apparently born a Brahmin in South India about 150 A.D. and lived for perhaps sixty years. According to K. Satchidananda Murty, he inspired the building of many temples, had the Bodhi tree and temple at Bodhagayā surrounded with a stone edifice with ornamental lattices, and inspired the stupa at Amaravati to be enclosed in a railing that has been called "the most voluptuous and most delicate flower of Indian sculpture."[6] In his survey *Twenty-Five Hundred Years of Buddhism,* P. V. Bapat calls Nāgārjuna "a philosophical thinker who has no match in the history of Indian philosophy, the greatest dialectician the world has ever seen." Thomas Berry, in his volume on Buddhism in the *Twentieth Century Encyclopedia of Catholicism,* says that Nāgārjuna may well be "the most influential single thinker known to the Asian world," and Karl Jaspers devotes his final chapter to him in *The Great Philosophers.* T. R. V. Murti thinks of him as a great turning point in the history of the oldest of the great international traditions, and according to Daisaku Ikeda, except for the labors of Nāgārjuna "the voluminous writings of Buddhism would not have reached China and Japan in nearly as systematized a form as they did."[7]

Some of the controversies that have always surrounded this famous Buddhist philosopher have rather obvious reasons, such as the lack of historical data on which a biographical account of his activities might be based. Beyond general agreement that he lived between 150 and 250 A.D., he is chiefly a legendary character in a drama that bears much the same relation to concrete historical fact as a masquerade bears to real life. Efforts of Walleser in our own time[8] and Kumarajiva's attempt centuries ago clearly indicate that any biography of Nāgārjuna may be beyond all believing. There have even been suggestions that more than one person was writing under the same name. His historical reality, in fact, has been questioned, just as it has been in the case of Vimalakirti, of whom it has been said that "outside of the *sutra* that carries his name we have no evidence to indicate that he ever existed."[9] Doubts like these, of course, have long been associated with Socrates, Shakespeare, and even Jesus of Galilee in the West. The texts of Nāgārjuna, however, have a distinguishable dialectical style, and further historical concreteness is acquired by the fact that he is always addressing himself to some adversary in the schools and schisms that flourished during the first five or six hundred years of Buddhism's existence.

Controversy surrounds Nāgārjuna's work not only because of the myth and legend left in his wake but also because of the lack of complete textual evidence for what he intended to say. "All the relevant material," Herbert V. Guenther writes, "has been lost in the original Sanskrit, and the Tibetan material remains mostly untouched." According to Lindtner, only thirteen of the dozens of texts associated with Nāgārjuna's name can be accepted as genuine; all the rest are either "probably not authentic" or spurious in nature.[10] In the absence of decisive information about his historical existence and the small percentage of writings that can be considered authentic, Nāgārjuna's perspectives and role in the development of Buddhism are viewed in many quarters as very obscure.[11]

Still a third reason for the endless controversy that has raged around Nāgārjuna's head is the apparently irresistible temptation of leading scholars to use him to support positions they wish on other grounds to hold and to confirm certain assumptions of traditions in which they have been reared. Illustrations abound. Jaspers, for example, sees Nāgārjuna as "expounding an original knowledge of what transcends all history and the limits of all linguistic and cultural systems."[12] Only in Wittgenstein does Jaspers find "an inkling of what it might mean to carry thought to the limit where it shatters," but only in Nāgārjuna does he find the struggle that he himself considers essential, the struggle "to think the unthinkable and to say the ineffable; Nāgārjuna knows he is doing this and tries to unsay what he has said."[13]

The classical illustration, however, of this barrier to understanding Nāgārjuna's work is the long effort of Indian philosophers to find in the great Buddhist writer a confirmation of their ancient teachings. Leading scholars have refused to set Nāgārjuna's Buddhism apart from the mothering matrix of Upaniṣadic thought. In a recent doctoral dissertation, Chandradhar Sharma, professor of philosophy at Banaras Hindu University, concludes that Nāgārjuna and Advaita Vedanta "are not two opposed systems of thought but only different stages in the development of the same central thought." Not to see this, Sharma says, is the source of the widespread misunderstanding of Buddhism today.[14] This continues the traditional posture toward Buddhism that Radhakrishnan wrote a quarter century before: "It is a strange irony that the great exponents of the two doctrines look upon themselves as supporting antagonistic positions." It is apparent, however, that Radhakrishnan's ground rules exclude all process thinking, whether in Heraclitean, Buddhist, or modern American form. "We mean by real," he writes, "any entity which has a nature of its own *(svabhāva)*, which is not produced by causes, which is not dependent on anything else. The real is the independent uncaused being. . . . It cannot be that Nāgārjuna treated the world as unreal and yet believed in no other reality. If all thought is falsification, there must be a real that is falsified. For, if there be no truth, then falsehood loses its meaning. . . . There is no relative knowledge without absolute knowledge being immanent in it. There is nothing empirical which does not reveal the transcendental. We cannot understand the transcendental reality except through the world of experience."[15] A more anti-Buddhist reading of Nāgārjuna's central points can hardly be imagined.[16]

Following Nāgārjuna's death, his most famous disciple, Āryadeva, "attacked other schools so harshly," as Hajime Nakamura writes, "that he was hated and finally assassinated." During the Gupta Dynasty (320–500 A.D.), the Japanese historian of Indian Buddhism continues, "Buddhism was so ignored that Buddhist temples were pulled down and building materials obtained thereby were used for the erection of Hindu temples."[17] While much of the endless argumentation was carried on in an atmosphere of searching out the truth, tolerance gave way with the appearance of Śaṅkara, who flourished during the eighth or ninth century A.D. "The more we examine the Buddhist system," he writes, "the more it gives way like a well dug in sand. It has no solid foundation. There is no truth in it. It can serve no useful purpose. Therefore all persons who desire the Good should at once reject Buddhism."[18] Śaṅkara gave the final deathblow to Buddhist philosophy in India by viewing it as a nihilistic system. Buddhism was ousted from the land of its birth by 1000 A.D., forced to find cultures outside India in which the insights of its founder could be understood in their own integrity. Until its nineteenth-century revival in India with Dharmapala and the Mahabodhi Society, Buddhism was forced to find its destiny elsewhere. For a thousand years the denial of any immutable substantial self, the affirmation of change with no substance undergoing the change, and the proposal that reality is a social process "empty" of anything transcendent or with independent existence—the core of the Four Noble Truths, the Noble Eightfold Path, and the Doctrine of Dependent Origination—would be free to win the hearts and minds of millions who were not predisposed to view them, in the manner of Chandradhar Sharma, as not only congenial to the Upaniṣadic teachings but actually borrowed from it.[19]

Of all the systematic international orientations, none has been more critical than Buddhism of the greatest barrier to constructive social change—the philosophical appeal to a transcendent reality outside nature not subject to empirical analysis and test. This refusal of rationality has never found any operational base in Buddhist thought, although efforts continue to interpret Nāgārjuna within the framework of Vedantic thought. Vedantic influence, to say the least, is seen in Ramanan's continued reference in his discussion of Nāgārjuna's philosophy to what is "undivided, unconditioned, ultimate, transcendent, eternal, the very real nature of all that is." One may applaud this author's focus on the central Buddhist point: "To cut at its root the tendency to cling to the specific as ultimate is the deepest truth of the denial of self which the Buddha taught. In its general form this is the error of misplaced absoluteness."[20] The reader, however, is left to wonder what might be the "absoluteness" that is not misplaced.

Śūnyatā may be considered the entire purpose of Ramanan's book on Nāgārjuna, an attempt to lay bare the different meanings of this most basic concept, "its devoidness of self-being, of unconditioned nature; this means the non-substantiality of the elements of existence; this means the ultimately true nature of things, the non-conceptual, non-phenomenal, undivided, indeterminate nature of the absolute, ultimate reality; śūnyatā also means the sense of the beyond, the thirst for the real, the thirst for fulfillment, which is the seat and spring of all the activities of man." And again, "thirst for the real is my rendering for seeking, longing." For Ramanan, *pratitya-samutpāda* refers "to the mundane nature of things, not the highest truth; the unconditioned and unchanging nature is not true in regard to the mundane nature of things."[21] All of this reference to an "unconditioned" reality not influenced by the mundane nature of things, an unutterable ultimate devoid of determinate characters, might well be construed as moving within the framework of Vedantic thought, rather than the more empirical, pragmatic, present-centered, democratic emphasis upon the concrete closeness to reality that characterizes Nāgārjuna's *Mūlamadhyamakakārikā* and the Buddha's teachings. According to Ramanan, *śūnyatā* is "the ultimate truth, the unconditioned undivided being which is the ultimate nature of the conditioned and the contingent."[22] Such are the consequences of failing to understand Buddhism as process thinking, indeed, as the most revolutionary philosophical discovery to appear until America's Whiteheadian, Peircean thought.

Beyond the originality of his writings on the relation between language and reality, the nature of logical fictions, and the absurdity of an unchanging Absolute in a changing world, Nāgārjuna has the two qualifications Hartshorne considers essential in the first-class philosopher: he is a rigorous logician, and he has "a sharp sense for the non-logical side of awareness."[23] His dialectic moves between the logic of abstractions and the momentary individualized concreteness of our direct encounter with life, where the reality of our experience is given from the depths of things, quite apart from any conceptual apprehension of what is really going on. "Premises are abstract, simplified outlines," as Hartshorne says, "and so are conclusions, while experiences are concrete and completely particularized." Ramanan makes the same point: "To set free the sense of the real from its moorings in abstractions is the chiefmost mission of the farer on the Middle Way." "All the abstract notions that make up what is called the world," Guenther writes, "hold men and women in deep sleep,"[24] but for Nāgārjuna the balanced intensity of experience needs no philosophical or theological support; it has positive structure and value as the fundamental chaos-transcending point in the creative advance of life itself.

Junjirō Takakusu calls Nāgārjuna's method the "Principle of Exhaustive Demonstration of Truth," exhausting all possibilities of an argued question and aiming like an arrow at disclosing out of the deeps of experience the free flow of "a state of undifferentiated indeterminateness." As Hemanta Kumar Ganguli says in his remarkable treatise on epistemology in early Indian philosophy, "The real is the pin-point particular of the moment, while the linguistic meaning is always a fictional construct which is called a universal." Vidushekhara Bhattacharya agrees: "Nāgārjuna strives to express the Inexpressible." Nāgārjuna in fact focuses our attention, Puligandla writes, "on the keen awareness of the limitations of all thought-constructions of reality, on the one hand, and direct, nonperceptual, nonconceptual, intuitive insight into reality on the other." The ultimate appeal in Buddhism is direct experience, which is, as Hartshorne says, "incomparably richer than our understanding can clearly grasp, no matter how much dialectic we engage in."[25] Nāgārjuna is one of the few philosophers in the entire history of thought who has not waged a relentless war against the currents of quality with which an individual's life is literally full.

Nāgārjuna therefore opposes himself to the tendency of civilized men and women to look for intellectual certitudes that no amount of empirical experience can ever call into question, the tendency to turn their backs on their own firsthand original experience in its unverbalized flow. "The elucidation of immediate experience," Whitehead writes, "is the sole justification for any thought, and the starting-point for all thought is the analytic observation of components of this experience."[26] Men and women, Nāgārjuna holds, as individuals and as social classes, will attempt to use rational structures for social control only at the risk of becoming victims of their noblest ideals.

The aim here is to relate men and women directly to the essenceless, selfless, individualized, and original experience, before any special zone of sense perception or abstract concept can lock them into the cultural membrane in which they have been reared. "The term 'non-self,'" Hajime Nakamura writes, "was explained as 'Substancelessness' (niḥsvabhāvatā). It is also called 'reality.'"[27] Reality in its "inexpressible" dimensions is encountered directly and concretely; it cannot be conceptualized at all.

Two things save Nāgārjuna from the charge of irrationalism.

First, he is using concepts in their evocative function, as search-lights for deepening awareness, rescuing people from cultural and academic clichés. We become more intelligent and responsible participants by probing into the unexplored depths of experience as it occurs in the momentary now. This deepened awareness of reality is something for which we have, in Ramanan's phrase, "a living thirst."[28] Secondly, Nāgārjuna is maintaining a sharp distinction between experience prior to sensory and conceptual form and the interrelatedness of a creative self-surpassing world: "O monks, he who sees the *pratītya samutpāda* sees the *Dharma*."[29] Creativity, Guy Welbon says, "pervades both the way and the goal of Buddhism, ignoring which would be to imperil any attempt to understand the one unambiguous distinction between Buddhism and Hinduism in most of its forms." "Though nonsensuous and nonconceptual," this creativity is, for Karl Potter, "rational in the sense that it is developed through a rational procedure." Nāgārjuna has avoided what Whitehead calls "the major vice of the intellect" — "the intolerant use of abstractions. Faith in reason springs from direct inspection of the nature of things as disclosed in our own immediate present experience. To experience this faith is to know that our experience, dim and fragmentary as it is, yet sounds the utmost depths of reality."[30] It is rational to refute wrong views, of course, but it is also rational to refuse to put other views in their place. Men and women cannot thereby become attached to those most subtle of all vehicles for the control of behavior (under the guise of searching for truth).

With rigorous logic Nāgārjuna formulates his concept of *śūnyatā* — the interrelatedness of existence — in such a way that its existence or nonexistence becomes a dead issue. He removes the question of existence from the area of debate. From his point of view, nothing is more important than to arrive at a clear understanding of a universe that is forever surpassing itself in every momentary now, but to argue about its existence is a waste of time. Worse than that, it reinforces that intellectual clinging that lies at or near the center of our major problems.

Everything exists only instantaneously; there is no abiding substance; whoever has missed the novelty of this world has missed everything. "Nāgārjuna's criticism of the 'own nature,'" Warder writes, "constitutes the basis of his entire work and is the best chapter for students to read first."[31] Nothing appears that is produced by either itself or another thing; everything appears by the operation of multiple causes and manifold conditions acting together to produce the momentary now. "Whether we are aware of it or not," according to David-Neel and Yongden, "the thoughts, the desires, the needs which we feel for life, our thirst for it — nothing of all this is completely ours, for all of it is collective, it is the flowing river of incalculable moments" having their source in the "interrelatedness that has no beginning and no conceivable end."[32] There is feeling but none who feels, change but no "ultimate reality" that undergoes the change, suffering but none who suffers; there are no thinkers but the thoughts, all of which are rooted in feeling, as Hume was the first Western philosopher to see. It is a selfless world of dynamic becoming, the causes of whose cooperative creativity are, in Takakusu's words, "boundless and limitless in a harmonious whole." Each passing moment is an occasion of experience, an emergent synthesis, which Whitehead immortalized in his famous aphorism "the many become one and are increased by one."[33]

These spontaneous individualized moments that preserve the past and go beyond it are the ground floor of *all* human and non-human existence, the implicit or explicit subject matter of *all* thought that understands itself. It is from these momentary experiences that all other unities are in some way derived. If each moment could speak, it would say, "It does not yet appear what we shall be." No conceivable deity could have conceptual knowledge of such individualized concreteness. Concrete individuality can never be conceptualized; it is creative. Philosophers and deities and other interested parties must all await the outcome of the passing moment as it leaves one center of relatedness to contribute its fullness to those yet to come. If we wished for some pathological reason to suppress awareness of real life, producing zombies for purposes of social control, no more effective means could be found than simply to domicile men and women in the dictionary and teach them to classify every experience in accordance with a categorial system. This is the thrust of Nāgārjuna's dialectical method. He leaves his reader speechless, but he opens human experience to the creativity that is beyond belief.

In opting for this unverbalized flow in its concreteness, Nāgārjuna becomes one of the first object lessons in the history of philosophy for avoiding Whitehead's famous "fallacy of misplaced concreteness." What we experience is the unthought vividness of life, not a conceptualizable substance or soul, and it is the aim of Nāgārjuna's philosophy to give importance to this vividness of the passing moment. Each passing moment is an occasion of experience with its own unity, an emergent synthesis that bears the trademark of the flashes of energy out of which it comes. Many times a second these "multiple energies," as David-Neel and Yongden call them, are creating their slight additions to the mass of memories and habits which constitute our character.[34]

In his category of Firstness, Peirce himself confirms the remark of a leading Buddhist scholar, A. K. Warder, "that the moments of the experienced *now* are the elementary qualities which are not analyzable into anything else, something that anyone can verify for himself."[35] "What the world was to Adam," Peirce writes, "on the day he opened his eyes to it, before he had drawn any distinctions, or had become conscious of his own existence—that is first, present, immediate, fresh, new, initiative, original, spontaneous, free, vivid, conscious and evanescent."[36] Daisetz Suzuki may have had the same point in mind in saying that Adam saw the animals before he named them.

"One is immediately conscious of his or her feelings," Peirce writes, "but not that they are feelings of an ego—the self is only inferred; there is no time in the present for any inference at all."[37] No Buddhist, including Nāgārjuna, has ever said it better. It may be difficult to see that what is experienced is always temporally prior to the experiencing, as Hartshorne argues,[38] but it becomes obvious when a hunter fires a shot far down the valley and we see the flash of his firing moments before we hear the explosion. A ray of light passing through the photo-electric cell to turn on the lights at the 1936 Chicago World's Fair had left the star Arcturus forty years before, on the date of the previous World Exposition in the same city. Enormous distances separating us from the stars confirm what Tibetan Buddhists perceived in such matters.[39] It is also what our memory teaches us every day.

For Peirce, furthermore, all thinking is dialogic in nature,

extending the feelings of the thinker into the feelings of others—
this is what he means by the "outreaching identity" of the self.[40]
What distinguishes the human mind is not that it is unextended
—nothing really is, Gilbert Ryle's "ghost in the machine" notwithstanding.[41] What distinguishes the mind is the acuteness of its
sensitivity to the shared processes of feeling and the equally distinctive ability to extend the range of our awareness by high-level
sign language, "by knowing which," Peirce says, "we know something more" and engage in dialogue with private and public
moments in our experience. This is crucial for Peirce's philosophy
of science, as well as an access road into profound dialogue with
the Buddhist orientation. "There is an immediate community of
feeling between parts of mind infinitesimally near together,
between the self at one moment and the oncoming self of the
next; without this," Peirce writes, "it would have been impossible
for minds external to one another ever to become coordinated in
the search for public truth to which even the most prejudiced persons will come if they pursue their inquiries far enough."[42] The
alternative is that each person will be the victim of narrowness,
as Peirce says, a "little prophet," a "crank," a "victim" of the "ghost
in the machine."[43] This is process philosophy in its American
form: "All origination is private. But what has been thus origi-
nated, publicly pervades the world."[44]

In ways rendered somewhat more definite and unambiguous by
Peirce, the dialectic of Nāgārjuna is a way of discovering that the
unthought is not the same as the unreal. Peirce is one of the few
philosophers, East or West, who has been utterly clear on the concreteness in comparison with which everything else is abstract.
With amazing persistence, he argues that a linguistic system does
the very opposite of what most philosophers and members of the
lay public assume: language does *not* bring together in fellow-
feeling and compassion what has been split, or for all practical
purposes evacuated by cultural metaphor and myth. To live by
linguistic signs is to live the falsification of the concrete, unthought fullness of our original experience. Efforts to find common ground in abstractions, rather than in areas of experience
such as shared hunger, serve more to tear into shreds our intuitive awareness of fellow-creatures. As Whitehead says, "It is easier
for general beliefs to destroy emotion than to generate it."[45] Men

and women who are fragmented and torn in their mutual awareness by such devious ways of locating common ground are not
healed with any kind of mere believing. People reared in "cultures
of belief," as Robert Bellah calls them,[46] are already predisposed to
turn life upside down, deriving the concrete from the abstract,
the contingent from the necessary, and modeling deity as the
absolute, infinite, eternal, and necessary being totally different
from creatures who, with the odds heavily against them, seek
amid an uncaring world to shape their precarious lives together.
These are some of the reasons why religions, as Whitehead puts
it, "are so often more barbarous than the civilizations in which
they flourish."[47]

In ways that proved decisive in distinguishing Buddhism from
its Upaniṣadic background, Nāgārjuna reasserts in analytical
form the revolution introduced by the historical Buddha seven
centuries before, the revolution that results when individuals
manage to become open and responsive to the inexhaustible creativity of the world. Nāgārjuna opens individuals to a world that is
held together by no perspective, a world that does not become
accessible by the mere changing of a point of view. People reared
in Western "cultures of belief," however, face almost insurmountable barriers when they try to relate directly to their own experience in the way Nāgārjuna suggests, partly because experience
in the West has usually been construed as a form of cognition, as
in Kant's way of viewing experience as our theoretical knowledge
of whatever is the case (produced by the forms of understanding)
or in Hegel's concept of experience as the dialectical movement
that consciousness exercises on itself as the Absolute Spirit
makes itself known.[48]

In honoring the principle of contrast and exalting it to the position of World Spirit, Hegel may have intended to assert the impos-
sibility of saying the deepest truths in consistent language; if so,
he was anticipated in this by Nāgārjuna more than seventeen centuries before, without the optimism, however, that is intrinsic to
Hegel's type of dialectic, which, as Nietzsche objected, "sees a
triumph in every syllogism, under the illusion that thought
might plumb the farthest abysses of being and even correct it."[49]
Despite his intention to avoid the merely intellectual or abstract
and substitute a more realistic notion of the self-consciousness of

humankind, Hegel's solution is another concept, ultimately the self-differentiating, self-bifurcating, self-alienating "I" which he considers the soul of the world. Unlike the Anglo-American Whitehead, with whom he is recently being compared, Hegel is not really interested in the concrete experience of the actual human being. He seems to be saying that it is the mind that unifies one passing moment with the next.

To say the very least, it is much more of a mystery in Hegel than in either Nāgārjuna or Whitehead how the ultimate contrasts are unified. For Nāgārjuna, reality in all of its unthought concreteness has its own social structure, the concrete relatedness called *śūnyatā*. There is no ontological core determining what any moment will be. Appearances to the contrary, Hegel's philosophy of self-consciousness is another in a long line of efforts on the part of Europe's most brilliant minds to turn people away from the concreteness of their experience, inducing them to view themselves in the mirror of abstractions. Whatever may have been his intentions, Hegel finds us in a linguocentric predicament and leaves us there, underestimating the capacity of language to break through the limits of its own past. Nāgārjuna, on the contrary, uses his dialectic in a positive way to bring his adversaries face to face with the unthought underside of experience. This is what Nāgārjuna's dialectic is all about.

Experience in the dominant philosophers of the West has never been accepted in its rich qualitative concreteness as it renews our life in the world. Until our own time, the West has been unable to free itself from nonprocess perspectives—philosophies of consciousness—which turn their backs upon the immediately experienced, aesthetically breathtaking, rich, and intense momentary nows. Non-Buddhist orientations of this kind generate the subject-object duality of thought and thing, mind and body, self and world, spirit and matter, man and nature, time and eternity, fact and value, that no amount of dialectic has ever been able to heal. This is another reason why, as Whitehead told Northrop when the latter was a graduate student in London, "we cannot be too suspicious of ordinary language, whether in philosophy or everyday life."[50] The ordinary language of "cultures of belief" throws our aesthetic, individualized, concrete, spontaneous, and novel experience out of nature as something that must be forgotten if we are to find common ground with our fellow-creatures. Northrop comments on how difficult it is for men and women reared in the West to think about an undifferentiated "Firstness" in life's qualitative flow, when all their lives they had thought about the world in terms of "facts" and "knowledge" differentiated by the mind.[51]

Process philosophies, on the other hand, use words as searchlights, probing the experience of experience, the feeling of feeling, "the sympathy whereby the world achieves its solidarity," as Hartshorne has recently written. "To perceive as we do," Hartshorne says, "is to intuit a part of the world as implicating the rest."[52] This implicate order of the world, as David Bohm, one of the West's leading physicists, has recently written,[53] is achieved by social feelings at various levels, in the nervous systems of animals, in the more loosely organized molecules of trees and rocks, in the feelings that relate the amoeba and other simple organisms to their environment, and in the more subtle social relationships linking the human creature into the vastness of a living world.

Nāgārjuna returns us to the dynamics of our own becoming, to reality as a social process, no element of which is either separate, independent, or of a self-established nature. There is not first a permanent subject and then an experience it adds to the storehouse of its past. "There is no entity anywhere that arises from itself, from another, from both (itself and another), or by chance" —this is the opening verse of Nāgārjuna's magnum opus, the *Mūlamadhyamakakārikā*. The world of what is really real is the result of the *non*existence of any independent self-established substance. It is *empty* of self-existence *(śūnyā)*, Nāgārjuna shows, because of the relational origination that makes all integrating possible. This *emptiness* of any self-established entity is what the world is full of, as Lama Anagarika Govinda says, "nothing existing but only in relationship to others."[54]

This is the point at which Indian Vedantists rejected Nāgārjuna's work as nihilistic, because a world that is creative and at the same time preservative—the core of process thinking—was beyond their comprehension; there had to be something that was independent of such change, something not subject to the self-surpassing impact of novel togetherness in the momentary now. For Vedantists in their ancient and modern mentalities, a substantial transcendent Being was essential.[55]

This view of reality as social process, variously called *pratitya samutpāda* or *śūnyatā* (translated as "conditioned genesis," "dependent" or "relational origination," "voidness," and "nothingness") "refers to the arising of a novel moment," Inada writes, "impelled by a natural dynamics of its own. It is a basic concept of all Buddhist traditions whether of the Theravāda or Mahayāna [or Vajrayāna]."[56] By virtue of *śūnyatā* there is that sense of power, vitality, quality, freedom, and self-active creativity with which everything begins. The Buddha's Enlightenment is the tremendous experience of this; it is not an intellectual matter but a full and vivid participation in the life of the whole world, experiencing its uninterrupted flow directly without the intervention of conscious thought.

Nāgārjuna, like the Buddha before him, is trying to return human thinking from abstractness to the concreteness from which thoughts obtain whatever meaning they acquire. His fundamental aim is seen in his remark that "those who cling to the 'emptiness only' view are incurable."[57] To quote the *Kāśyapa Parivarta*, "Of all theories, *Śūnyatā* is the antidote. Him I call the incurable who mistakes *Śūnyatā* itself as a theory *(dṛṣṭi)*. . . . It is as if a drug, administered to cure a patient, were to remove all his disorders, but were itself to foul the stomach by remaining therein. Would you, Kāśyapa, consider the patient cured? Likewise, Kāśyapa, *Śūnyatā* is the antidote for all dogmatic views; but him I declare incurable who misapprehends *Śūnyatā* itself as a theory."[58] "The fact of dependent origination," Lindtner writes, "is exactly what you think of as emptiness, but if someone believes in that [emptiness] he is lost." According to Alicia Matsunaga, furthermore, it has not been as unusual as one might think for Buddhist scholars "to cling to a view of *śūnyatā*, endowing it with a reality reminding one of another kind of *atman*." (The same point was being made about nirvana during my year at U Nu's ill-fated International Institute for Advanced Buddhistic Studies in Rangoon.) Nāgārjuna's critique of the adversary's position on this issue is an attempt, Inada says, "to de-ontologize his realistic tendencies. But his critique does not end there. He will not leave his opponent suspended in so-called deontologized mid-air. Like all true Buddhists, he will try his best to return the deontologized nature back to solid grounds, i.e., in constant contact with true reality, without the traces or vestiges of the mind's imposition on reality as such *(tattva)*. Deontologization is at best a half-way measure, a conceptual device, that needs to be brought back to the full experiential content of the total process."[59]

In Buddhism, therefore, according to Nāgārjuna, reality in all of its unthought concreteness has its own social structure, the concrete relatedness called *śūnyatā*. There is no ontological core determining what any moment will be. Each event as a novel form of togetherness is an addition to the old, a momentary now unifying itself with whatever has been relevant in the past, but passing beyond it to something new. Each event is both caused by the past and free from the past, free in the creativity that pervades the world.

The world as understood in Nāgārjuna and all forms of Buddhism is a creative world, its "one unambiguous distinction from Hinduism in most of its forms."[60] Enriched by the contributions of the past, but developing in unpredictable ways, the future is open. Everything that happens is partly constituted by past events —the past is incarnate in the passing now—but, as Hartshorne states in a discussion of Nāgārjuna's philosophy, "every moment of life we assume more or less consciously that the future is a matter of options, possibilities, limited by certain impossibilities and necessities."[61] If we do not know, though, what possibility (irreducible to necessity) is, we know nothing much about Buddhism's teaching of the interrelatedness of existence, or dependent origination *(śūnyatā* or *pratītya-samutpāda)*. It is therefore a mistake to understand Nāgārjuna as committing the fallacy of misplaced symmetry (that is, embracing the fallacious belief that the past and future determine the present in equal degrees). Buddhist behavior implies a real past, a capacity for self-correction, and thus a merely potential future in which the suffering might be diminished. Becoming grows in this *asymmetrical* way. "Time's arrow" is taken far more seriously in Buddhism than in Hinduism, as the succession of fleeting moments, the present one being increased to become a future that is new. Any possible experience is *always* being overtaken and increased by a new experience.

Whatever cannot be overtaken in this way, whatever cannot be increased with a novel form of awareness, would be the permanent, substantial, transcendent Being that Buddhism and *all* other process philosophies reject.[62]

What emerges is creative and at the same time preservative. Nothing is ever lost; the novel one embraces the antecedent many; the new, more definite, fleeting now includes the multiplicity. Each event is thus what Buddhism calls the "ripening fruit" of the past, each the "heir" of its own actions, inheriting the past but free in a nondeterministic world of relational origination. "The concept of *karma*," Inada reminds us, "is not indigenous to Buddhism, but here it is transformed into a non-deterministic action concept," to become a succession of self-creative acts "that propel the wheel of life." For Buddhism, as for Peirce, the past is the sum of accomplished facts, but, as Hartshorne states, "there are new facts every moment, new additions to the past; becoming is *creation* of concrete actualities, not their destruction. Truth changes only by additions, not subtractions."[63] In Hartshorne's judgment, Buddhism comes closer than Heraclitus to this novel insight.

Each of the interrelated moments in Nāgārjuna's *śūnyatā* is creatively synthesized in a process that is given a more detailed analysis and formulation in Whitehead's revolutionary concept of prehension. "The Buddhists, who first held this view," Hartshorne writes, "spoke of 'dependent origination.' Change for Buddhism is the coming to be of new actualities. It is not one entity different at different times, but different entities or single events, one after another. Whitehead takes this view, and may have done so before knowing about Buddhism, which also provides for this connectedness of events. Self-identity is this relation of the present moment with the past. To have seen this so long ago is the glory of Buddhism." In an experience many past events "become one and are increased by one"; it is no accident that in a world thus endlessly and inexhaustibly creative the Buddhist orientation found no role for the conventional views of God.[64]

These novel moments, these upsurges in our individualized experience, shake the world free from the grip of its past; it is these that also shake us free from our social paradigms and categorial systems and lead us to a process view of what is going on.

This is the function of Nāgārjuna's famous *lemmas*—they direct attention to the unthought in its nonlogical thrust. What is unforgettable in Nāgārjuna, and perhaps his greatest single contribution to the Buddhist legacy, is his sharp appreciation of the difference between linguistic conceptual systems and the concrete individualized moments of existence, which, in Hartshorne's phrase, "exceed our powers of clear intuition." Stcherbatsky is perhaps the first of Buddhist scholars in the West to stress the positive reason why Nāgārjuna was "opposed to those systems, modern or ancient, which asserted the capacity of human reason to cognize things as they really are; he even presses this incapacity to the utmost and challenges the claims of logic with greater emphasis than any philosopher has ever done."[65]

Buddhism is centered in this kind of analysis of the experienced momentary nows, and for twenty-four centuries no idea has withstood scrutiny unless it could illumine the compulsions and the unexamined unconscious drives, particularly the temptation to seek the security and renewal of human life in something beyond or behind the succession of actual events. Wherever Buddhist perspectives have become habitual as a controlling style of life, reality is felt in each individual's experience as events linked *organically* (as forming wholes), causally, creatively in multiform relations, each actuality dependent upon predecessors and contemporaries, independent of nothing except the future yet to emerge.[66]

It is important to separate Buddhism from the Western mysticism some scholars find implied in the emphasis upon the individualized momentary now, spontaneous, original, and direct in its encounter with the world, and the dynamic community of life to which each moment belongs and in which it participates in ways beyond belief. What we are talking about in Buddhism is not the mysticism of Eckhardt, the Absolute of T. R. V. Murti and Ninian Smart,[67] nor what Edward Conze calls "the structure of the spiritual and intermediary worlds."[68] By rejecting rational structures as incapable of incorporating the deepest truth about our experience in the world, Nāgārjuna does not become a counterpart of the Western mystic. As Kamaleswar Bhattacharya says, "He seems to be a mystic, but he is not a mystic who renounces thought and its expression of language." He is, indeed, as I have indicated at some length, a rigorous logician. His "mysticism," if it may be so called, may bear some slight resemblance to that of Wittgenstein, who could say, "Not how the world is, is the mystical, but that it is."[69]

Nāgārjuna shows that what is fundamental, what is actually going on, is neither culture, nor linguistic systems, nor social classes, nor governments, nor any of the other abstract scaffoldings that seek to introduce immobility into the creativity that is the universal element in all reality. He shows that deeper than these self-centered encapsulated structures that separate individuals from one another at the deepest level of their individualized experience, the common bond that holds the world together is found in the self-creative feelings which are in every concrete actuality, finding corroboration in events that are closest to us in our participation in the common life. The subsequent history of Buddhism is a living witness that a system of orientation need not become fixated within a conceptual corral and that individuals of radically different ethnic, racial, social class, and cultural backgrounds can communicate and relate to one another on a level more fundamental than linguistic and cultural form. If this were not the case the outlook for the species would be dismal indeed. No ancestral tradition has ever had any defense against this deeper-than-cultural penetration beneath the overlay of sense data, conceptual metaphor, and conventional cliché. The meeting of Buddhism and other process philosophies in the contemporary world, therefore, can be expected to generate among rational men and women the ability to relate to the original experience of fellow-creatures on the crossroads of our new global existence.

# 5. Buddhism and Western Theology

*All the gods of history thus far may be viewed as a product of human arrogance, ignorance, and pride. It is creative interchange, not thought, that should command the ultimate commitment of faith. Visions of the universe change from age to age, and the creativity operating in human existence will provide new visions from time to time. What calls for ultimate commitment is not such visions, therefore, but the kind of interchange which creates appreciative understanding of the original experience of one another and the integration of each of what he or she gets from others in this way. Also, we have come to a time when science is continuously revolutionizing our view of the world. For reasons such as these we must live in the power and keeping of the creative transformation that expands our vision and not identify our faith with any one vision that happens to be most popular at the time.*

Henry Nelson Wieman, Intellectual Autobiography

*The idolatry of the eternal which has poisoned European theology since Greek times commits two fatal flaws: first, the fallacy that whatever is everlasting must also be eternal; and, second, the decision that the eternal is to be sought in the area of linguistic and cultural form, rather than in the natural continuity of momentary nows which are the ground floor of the living world. Things everlasting need not be eternal; they come into being but do not pass away, while things eternal always were and always will be. Both of these errors of Western theology have played a central role in the "death of God," which, except for these two flaws, might have been viewed as a foregone conclusion at least a century before it appeared.*

Charles Hartshorne, Creativity in American Philosophy

Of all intellectual pursuits none can match theology in its provincialism. In a universe that is always new, always advancing into novelty, in its actuality never the same twice,[1] Western theology in its dominant forms has refused to be drawn across the threshold into the twentieth century. The encounter and slow interpenetration of Buddhism with "the spirituality of the West," Langdon Gilkey says, "constitutes the major intellectual and religious event of our era," because it provides a situation entirely new "in which our gospel must be interpreted and through which it may become relevant and true for us again."[2] According to Gilkey, "Creative elements in our own heritage, long covered over and yet suddenly relevant to our new situation, are thereby uncovered."[3] But the theological base for the most part remains the same — possession of a sacred book in which a holy community is commissioned to persevere as agents of the divine, apparently in and through the nuclear holocaust now threatening the entire planet. This is the kind of theological provincialism that has prevailed in the West.

During the last century, however, a new "process" theology has been coming to the fore, a theology capable of a deeper and more creative encounter with the Buddhist orientation, a theology that knows that the most penetrating probes into what is fundamental and real, the greatest suffering, the transforming compassion, the sense of an intuitive love that holds the universe together — all are imprisoned when men and women are taught to interpret their experience in the symbols and framework of a sacred book. Whitehead has put this central theme of process theology in explicit terms: "It is therefore a vicious regress to control life, communication, memory, aspiration, and hope under the dictates of a linguistic and cultural system."[4] Grounded in the aesthetic power base of the rich individualized experience of momentary nows, this new theology has freed itself from the apparently incurable need of the ancestral Western tradition to place experience under conceptual lock and key.

Where Buddhism differed from all Western theology until a century and more of process thinking created a new alternative outlook is in the persuasion that what is ultimately real in our experience is best left unconceptualized, instead of becoming another in the long treasury of abstractions associated with the divine. Apart from this theological asceticism, all forms of asceticism constitute one falsification or another of that mysterious experiential background which Wittgenstein confessed himself unable to express.[5]

The aim throughout Buddhism's centuries of development has been to demonstrate in practice how individuals can participate directly in what is most real in their experience, eliminating through meditation the false selves and the tyranny of language that are the major barriers to the celebration of life.[6] "There is nothing in the teachings of Buddhism," Herbert Guenther writes, "which our immediate experience does not contain." Buddhism, Inada says, "is grounded in ordinary human nature and experience" and is "the most thorough-going naturalistic discipline the world has ever witnessed, though it is unappreciated in this light."[7]

This is precisely what process thinkers have been saying for more than a hundred years. It is quite amazing, indeed, that Buddhism and America's classical philosophers—Charles Peirce, William James, John Dewey, and Alfred North Whitehead—all agree across twenty-five centuries of radically different cultural experience that, as Whitehead says, "the foundations of the world are to be found, not in the cognitive experience of conscious thought, but in the aesthetic experience of everyday life."[8]

What comes to the fore as the idolatry of the West falls away is what Hartshorne refers to as "the need to be free from theory": "We have to respond to situations always more complex than we can understand, and we have to respond with more than understanding. Buddhist meditation has this as its purpose. We might begin with the importance of nonconceptual, nontheoretical apprehension of reality."[9] With such pronouncements as these closing words of an essay entitled "Toward a Buddhisto-Christian Religion," which reflects Hartshorne's career-long reading of Buddhism, the provincialism of Western theology begins to come to an end, as it does with Dewey's call for a "reconstruction in philosophy." Dewey, who argues for an end to the traditional Western fascination with the supposedly immutable and fixed truth, observes that human experience is much richer than the limited forms in which it has been given linguistic expression in the West and that "where egotism is not made the measure of reality and value, we are citizens of a vast world beyond ourselves with which a sufficiently experimental probing may give us a sense of unity."[10]

An explosive process of global interaction is, in fact, drawing men and women out of their ancient linguistic chambers, out of the conceptual systems which for several centuries Western nations have imposed upon the modern world. (This struggle against a linguistically imposed provincialism is central in my chapter on Nāgārjuna.) Language, whether centuries old or modern, and whether Eastern or Western in origin, is *not* to be accepted simple-mindedly as being neutral or noncommittal in dealing with the ultimate nature of the world. To speak of any self-established entity, any person or substance, as having an identity within itself, is to use words to spread confusion. To cure ourselves of the misuse of language, the ultimate appeal must be to the superior richness of the concrete momentary now, in relation to which everything is an abstract and incomplete entity. To remain positively open to the creative freedom of *śūnyatā*, Nāgārjuna insists, has always constituted the major challenge of the Buddhist orientation. Buddhism thus frees individuals from the kind of sacred scriptures, ecclesiastical authority, and mandatory creed that have played such a central role in the West. The positive content of what remains is a religion of infinite compassion, without ritual, without theology in the traditional Western sense, without an inflexible belief system, and without an appeal to any reality beyond what can be found in the persisting probing of individualized experience.

Empirically sophisticated, democratic, pragmatic, Buddhism has always had its focus in the problem of suffering. One of the central discoveries of the historical Buddha is that suffering tends to be concealed by the holiest systems of belief. States of mind generated by theories of the divine have usually had the strange side effects of producing psychological and social states that displace the pursuit of truth. Reasoning beings, according to Buddhism, have a privileged place in nature only to the extent that they use their powers of thought and communication to widen and vivify the qualitative richness of experience in its spontaneous flow. It is here the ontological dimension of life is found, not in those substance-centered thought systems of the West that have been under attack from the beginnings of the modern world.

## The Crisis in Western Theology

To many of the West's most brilliant minds during the past two centuries or more, theology has become colloquial and superficial. It is no longer the foundation on which a culture can be based. In the overly dramatic terms of the post-Nietzsche era, theology has been shaken in its foundations by the death of God. Not a few of the leading critics have been theologians themselves, in their own way. Models of honesty and integrity, they have delivered the most devastating shock any organized religion has ever been forced to confront. It is one of the merits of the new process theology, however, that it is vulnerable to none of these powerful attacks upon Western religious foundations. It shares with Buddhism, indeed, those commitments that are best able to flourish in a world that has been "emptied" of the idolatries of the past.

Dietrich Bonhoeffer was the first to give contemporary expression to the radical thesis that the concept of God is a cultural concept and that no embodiment of the concept in human institutions can hope to incarnate reality in this way. To quote Bonhoeffer: "Now that it has come of age, the world is more godless, and perhaps it is for that very reason nearer to God than ever before." Bonhoeffer called this new concept "religionless Christianity." Among the American "death of God theologians," Thomas J. J. Altizer has edited a volume entitled *Toward a New Christianity: Readings in the Death of God Theology,* in which he incorporates essays by William Hamilton, Paul van Buren, Gabriel Vahanian, and others. Those named here are the major figures of the movement. All write on the thesis that we are witnessing the end of Christian culture, on the grounds that culture, as Nietzsche put it, is "all too human" to incorporate the divine in its linguistic system and social institutions. These men are but a few of "the Titans who storm heaven," as Whitehead writes, "armed with passionate sincerity, who destroy the religious systems of the past." They have been, Whitehead believes, the battering rams against the belief, not yet extinct, "that violence is the primary mode of sustaining large-scale social existence." They have belatedly awakened millions in the West to the fact that great social organizations throughout the history of Western Europe have been what Whitehead calls "contrivances for stunting humanity."[11]

The revolution in Western theology as suggested by these famous "Titans" is much broader in scope than historians have yet enabled us to understand, since it expresses itself in more subtle ways, such as in the writings of five of England's most prominent writers in recent times—Matthew Arnold, Robert Browning, Gerard Manley Hopkins, Emily Brontë, and Thomas De Quincey—all of whom often depict a world that has been abandoned by God.[12] It is apparent that something profound and far-reaching has happened to the capacity of people to believe in teachings formerly accepted without question. Uncounted millions are no longer under the guidance of the values on which their great civilization was thought to have been based. People living on the brink of the century of the great world wars had become like trees planted in the rich supportive soil in which their forebears had flourished, but they had now become unable to respond in the ancestral ways, because they had come to perceive an absolute fissure between their upreaching branches and the deep supportive soil. Alienated by the idolatries of the ancestral tradition, they were impervious to the awareness that, in Whitehead's words, "their experience, dim and fragmentary as it is, yet sounds the utmost depths of reality."[13]

People wearied with a theology beset with problems of such magnitude can be expected to welcome with open arms the creative encounter of Buddhism with the new process theology, both of which insist that what is of ultimate importance in human life is best left unconceptualized, first because life does not need to be shored up and justified by appeals to something beyond experience, and second, because any theological formulation is in large part a product of the linguistic and cultural membrane in which it is born.

Closer collaboration between Buddhism and this new process thinking will reinforce the mental and social magnanimity and emotional plenitude already characterizing men and women who find themselves participating in a global community without geographical, racial, ethnic, and religious limits.[14] Such collaboration will allow the direction and momentum of life to assert itself in its full depth and vividness, without any conscious intent to bring it about, and it will remove all doubt that the greatest struggle of humankind has never been against some other nation or race or social class, but against the compulsiveness and rigidity that blind individuals to the wonder of being alive. These two consummations of vast cultural experience over the past two or three millennia of history are capable in such collaboration of awakening men and women to more of the fullness of concrete quality streaming across their sinews and nerve-endings, enabling them to participate with deliberate intent in the creative advance of a new "civilization of experience," as my final chapter will describe it.

## The Human Sources of Religion

The over-simplified Western views of the content of religious experience that have dominated all Western societies until recently are now in the process of falling away. What is coming to the fore are deepening insights into certain experiences that reflect both the submerged profundities of human nature and the organic wholeness of the universe at large. When we penetrate the illusions regarding a substantive self, we find the residuary individualized and original feelings in a process that never ends. These feelings serve as windows into the nature of life in its human and more-than-human dimensions. They are the chief features of human experience that not only motivate the religious quest but keep it watered as though from an everlasting stream. An interpretation of human experience that leaves these features out of account cannot be said to describe the facts of life. Such features indicate in the most convincing way that religion is more deeply rooted in our everyday experiences than generally believed, growing out of sources Wordsworth might have said are "deeper than tears."

The first of these experiences of everyday life is the sense of being alone in the world, not in the physical sense of living away from people, but in the sense of being an infinitesimally small entity surrounded by a sea of influences not subject to our control. Blaise Pascal, the seventeenth-century mathematician and physicist, made this experience famous for Western readers. Some people know this feeling as a sense of being dwarfed by the complexity of large-scale social organizations with their concentrations of colossal power. Some know it as a feeling of being alone in the midst of the crowd, homeless though adequately housed, starved for more than food in the jumble of the daily news.

The second of these everyday facts of life that are taken into account in a religious ordering of our experience is the sense of being responsible, of being unable to hold other people and environmental factors completely accountable for behavior that is our very own. Out of the creativity of life itself, in the face of multitudes of causes narrowing our options, something is always left for the decision of the momentary now. Each present passing moment is both caused by the past and free from the past, free in the creativity that pervades the world. Such self-creative acts, in the Buddhist Way, "propel the wheel of life."[15] Individuals can never with complete equanimity turn their backs on the original experience that it is their natural roles to create. In the middle of each creative deed, the human organism is never certain what the choice of the instant will be. "Many times a second," Hartshorne writes, "we are creating something additional, however slight, in the mass of memories and bodily habits which makes up character, and always this addition is incompletely specified in advance by the prior causal conditions. Just now one is *almost*, but not entirely, the slave of causal necessities; yet by persistently leaning toward the better side of the causally open actions, we can — who knows how far — improve our character. We *can* do this. But we can also not do it."[16] We are, we feel, unavoidably our own responsible individuals, and we can never rest content with the suspicion that this is not the case.

The third feature of human experience in the artesian spring of religious inquiry is the experience of being a growing, changing, sometimes progressing, sometimes becalmed person, without ever being able or entirely willing to bring this process to a stop. Every moment is part of the creativity of life itself. Endless repetition and monotony are intolerable, even to people who may momentarily feel like saying, "Stop the world; I want to get off." It is part of the essence of human life that the range of our experience must be increasing in depth and scope. No one is ever "well adjusted" or perfectly fitted to his or her immediate past. Creative becoming, as the *Encyclopedia of Buddhism* says, is "the very essence of existence."[17]

The fourth of these experiences of everyday life that are the watering source of all religion is the sense of having a uniqueness that is almost universally overlooked, beneath the lip service with which it is honored. We know ourselves to be unrepeatable. We resent it when we think that this is being overlooked. There is a sense of being wounded in our self-respect and dignity whenever we have reason to suspect that others are ignoring the individuality we ourselves have similar tendencies to forget. People do us a high favor, and we feel this strongly, whenever they feel our original presence, and not merely as members of a social class, nation, racial, or ethnic group. Unfortunately, there are ancient religious communities still thriving in the modern world whose members feel vividly that they have no friend but their God.

The fifth, and in some ways the most important of all of these experiences of everyday life, is the sense of being unproductive, of having little or nothing to which we can point as evidence of our own work. Rote behavior and monotonous toil strip the sense of achievement from millions in the contemporary industrial system, but this is an experience rich in historical parallels—the sense of being wasted, of seeing our talents "lodged with us useless," our capabilities unwanted and ineffective, in what many have called "the pathology of unproductiveness."

The sixth experience functioning as the source of the religious quest is the need for wholeness and consistency (and the limited capacity we have for tolerating their opposites). In our private lives this need drives us toward integrity; in interpersonal relations it is known as love; in religion it is called "purity of heart," or "union with God." The striving for balance and wholeness as our experience proceeds is one of the deepest resources upon which we can count in healing the broken individual, the lost sense of identity, the feeling of futility and worthlessness. There is a passion in everyone toward completeness or fullness in what we seek and think and love: "Oh, to be fully engaged and wholly involved in whatever we find worth doing!"

Except in serious pathological states, there is in all of us the need to communicate our original experience to others—the seventh everyday experience motivating religion. We feel others as blessings who can be depended upon to be open to what we are experiencing, to accept us without distrust, and to receive the truth about us without threat of exploitation or betrayal. So strong is this need to communicate our original experience that blindness and deafness may fall together upon the same person without completely bringing the drive to communicate to an end.

The eighth of these common human experiences motivating religion comes to us in the form of questions we cannot avoid and cannot answer, questions indeed that no one can answer. We live in the grip of inadequate knowledge, surrounded with emergent situations to which past knowledge is not entirely applicable. The actions with which we must proceed have implications which can find full recognition only in retrospect: the owl of Minerva flies only at twilight, after the shades of evening have fallen, and, indeed, after we and our generation and even our nation have passed away.

The ninth of the facts that generate the religious life—the fear of death—is probably never consciously felt in its full intensity. No one can view with complete repose the termination of everything that gives meaning to life. The thought that death will render all our efforts meaningless in the end is perhaps too frustrating and painful to be permitted free and full and open acceptance. Unless there be something in us, or from us, that escapes the complete destruction and disintegration of death, the threat of meaninglessness haunts us to the end. Every religion everywhere has taken this fact of life into account.

The list of these everyday experiences that lie at the heart of the religious quest might be added to, or reduced in number. The point is not that there are nine, or five or four, but that they are powerful enough to keep religious inquiry alive everywhere on earth, though the quest may be given a different name. The deepest tragedy of the age of science and technology, of high-pressure existence in massive social organizations, is that a new condition of humanity has been spawned that tends to suppress and distort these poignant features of everyday life, inducing men and women, generation after generation, to lean upon authoritarian creeds, hierarchies in totalitarian systems, and the illusion that piled up material possessions can satisfy the deepest hunger of the human heart.

Because these nine common experiences can never be avoided

or completely suppressed, no truly religiously sensitive person is ever satisfied with his or her religion. To be satisfied with one's religion, indeed, is the tell-tale mark of a religion disoriented from what is really going on. It is possible, of course, for an individual to conceal for a limited number of years these vital human needs beneath the externalities of a purely conventional religion. The greatest honor that can be conferred upon Buddhism, however, is that it is an orientation capable of *meeting* the demands of all these common experiences of life: the fear of death, the need to communicate, the demand for wholeness and consistency, the need to protest our identity amid the overwhelming pressures of social conformity, the need to be responsible for acting in the light of what we are learning about ourselves, with anxiety acting in the twilight of insufficient knowledge and error, facing questions no one can answer, aware in some degree of the pathology of our own unproductiveness, and the fear of being dwarfed by the enveloping immensity of the universe in which we live.

In Buddhism all of these facts of everyday life constitute the source of the problem of suffering and the general unsatisfactoriness of life. Buddhism shares this with process theology, which is the culmination, Hartshorne writes, of three centuries of reconsideration of the proper meaning of the religious term "God."[18] To turn away from these new perspectives of process theology might well become the atheism of the immediate future, but this alternative is not entirely relevant to Buddhism, since without a theology it has oriented life to the creativity of the passing moment in forms of meditation that free individuals in their concreteness from the illusions of the false, self-aggrandizing glorifications that have characterized the dominant religions of the West. Though it is hardly irrelevant to Buddhist thinkers of the contemporary world that Buddhism arose at a time when a process theology comparable to Wieman's, or Dewey's, or Hartshorne's not only did not exist but was scarcely dreamed of in any clear conceptual form, the fact that the new alternatives of process theology have now reached their most systematic form constitutes a new basis for a more creative encounter between Buddhism and Whiteheadian-Hartshornean thinking than history has witnessed in the past.

## Theology Within the Limits of Experience

What I have called the crisis in Western theology and the nine features of everyday life that instigate the search for a religious system of orientation and devotion were in the forefront of the mind of Henry Nelson Wieman when he arrived at the University of Chicago in 1926 and proceeded to develop his "empirical theology" on what he thought of as the fifth level of cultural development in the long history of the species.[19]

The first level of this development in human culture is preoccupied with the necessities of biological survival, such as food, shelter, and reproduction. At the second level, people are not obsessed with biological survival to the same extent as in the first, but they live under the dictates of a religious tradition reputed to have acquired the truth from beyond the world. At the third level, where the unquestioned authority of a religious tradition has lost much of its power, leaving individuals to decide which of the available illusions they will accept, genuine religious inquiry is yet far in the future; acceptance of illusions and compulsive drives is near at hand. People, though, at the fourth level, begin to be badgered by a sense of the fundamental meaninglessness of their existence. The unsolved religious problem, which Wieman's empirical theology faces, has not yet come to the forefront of conscious awareness, but the doctrines, symbols, rituals, and traditional authoritative teachings have lost their force. Despite the powerful advances in productive technology, millions of men and women are still living at each of these levels. On the fifth level, however, the most highly developed people in the area of religion have commenced to wonder about the intrusions of science into all concerns with truth, and the new cultural threshold appears. Holding fast to cherished beliefs is rejected, not only in religion, but in all other concerns as well.

For Wieman, "The transition to the fifth level of cultural development is accomplished by redefining the problem of ultimate religious concern."[20] The question of religion is no longer whether anyone believes in God. It is no longer a question of recognizing the authority of the Bible. As Wieman pored over the writings of Charles Peirce, he was fired with the intent of *learning* more about the religious problem, instead of conceiving his work in divinity school as "teaching the Truth."[21] What form religion will take in the future we do not know, but as Wieman makes clear talk by theologians of "the death of God" is symptomatic of the new reformation at the fifth level of cultural development where empirical sciences join religion to cope with the new awareness that religion is ultimately a *question*, rather than a set of answers.

The religious question, Wieman says, is often conceived in ways that make empirical inquiry useless, such as asking what is the nature of Being as such, what is the meaning of existence in its totality, or what reality are we experiencing when we experience awe, wonder, mystery, and the Holy. The question Wieman considers of ultimate concern is this: What operates in human life as a process which transforms man as he cannot transform himself, freeing individuals from suffering and bringing them to maximum richness in the quality of life?[22]

What do we find in empirical inquiry when it is guided by this question? It is that the world as we experience it in everyday life is actually a myriad of events infinitely rich with quality. Quality is the substance of events; it is the ultimate reality. So abundant is the quality of any moment that no words can exhaust its fullness. If one does not accept richness of quality as the great good of life, one will scarcely be able to live at the human level with any assured satisfaction.[23] There is nothing more fundamental to the religious quest, therefore, than human experience — "we cannot go beyond it; what we experience is ultimate reality."[24] Nothing can contribute to religious inquiry unless we find it operating here in our lives, and it is here that we must deal with it.

The first step, Wieman writes in his "Intellectual Autobiography," is to repudiate belief and knowledge as ultimate sources of security and value. The second step is to recognize that the ultimate source of security and value is the concrete fullness of quality, which is never identical except in small part with the structures by which we know it. The third step, if one is to conduct religious inquiry with any hope of success, is to seek knowledge, not for any ultimate security it can yield, but as an instrument to guide conduct and disposition in dealing with that fullness of concrete reality that extends infinitely beyond the compass of knowledge.[25] The experience to which Wieman refers in the phase "the flow of felt quality" is the creativity that *transforms* the appreciable world. The main reason, however, that Wieman focuses attention on the creativity operative in human experience "and gives little attention to creativity operative elsewhere in the cosmos, is precisely because he sees with increasing clarity that the hope of all life, so far as we know anything about it, lies not in cells and atoms nor in any of the lower animals, but in the creative transformation of man both as individual, as a planetary society, and as a continuing history."[26]

Wieman left Harvard University in 1917, before the great Anglo-American philosopher Alfred North Whitehead arrived on the scene, but he later discovered in Whitehead's writings precisely what he wanted—a way of thinking in religion that mobilized science in its behalf. "By giving scientific demonstration to the principle of concretion," he wrote about Whitehead's work, "he is also establishing scientifically the creativity of the world."[27] Wieman, in fact, appropriated Whitehead's concept of concrescence, or prehension (what Whitehead describes as "the production of novel togetherness"), in his central concept of Creative Interchange, "the source of human good," the dynamic, self-surpassing integrating of the total experience of all entities of the world.

Creative Interchange becomes for Wieman a functional definition of God, "the event" on which everything in the universe depends. It is constituted by what he calls "four sub-events" always going on in experience at the human level: (1) the emergence of a new awareness of felt quality, (2) the integration of the newly emerged quality with those previously acquired, (3) the expansion of the appreciable world, and (4) the deepening of community between individuals resulting from these new meanings and integrations. These events, Wieman argues, face almost insurmountable obstacles in the way men and women presently are reared, but they insinuate themselves in the interstices of experience and come fully to the fore when individuals open themselves to their rich qualitative flow. Such experience becomes mystical when the wealth of quality is so great that the order required for conscious appreciation of what is going on cannot find appropriate forms of verbal communication.[28]

On the face of things, the four events are such that no one can deliberately bring them about: no one can give a new feeling of quality—it just happens; no one can acquire a new perception or perspective, nor add a cubit to his or her stature by taking thought; no one can integrate a new perspective with those already in one's apperceptive mass; no one can expand the appreciable world or deepen the existing community of life. All of these things emerge in the process of creative interchange between individuals and the rest of nature. For Wieman, "Man is made for creative transformation as a bird is made for flight. To be sure he is in a cage much of the time. The bars of the cage are the resistances to creative transformation which are present in himself and in the world round about. Resistances are encountered which bring on anxiety, frustration, failure, and misunderstanding. To avoid suffering, the mind becomes evasive and creativity dies down. The bird ceases to beat against the bars of the cage."[29] Millions of men and women, however, awaken and hear the beating of great wings. The truth has never lain on the surface of things.

Creative Interchange protects and nurtures the original experience of individuals. It is the process on which the richness of their lives depends, in the face of an otherwise overwhelming environment of social conformity and oppression. It is the interchange enabling individuals to prize the original experience of one another, in the relationship appropriately called love. It supports, in fact, the kind of behavior Buddhism has made famous in the ideal of the bodhisattva. Without knowing anything about Buddhism prior to the writing of his major books, and working exclusively with the materials and insights of the West, Wieman describes the bodhisattva ideal as well as it has ever been described: it is an integrative process of living that brings individuals into organic fellowship with one another, developing a matrix of mutual support and relatedness between all parts of the cosmos.

Wieman, indeed, shares with Buddhism many themes, not the least of which is his opposition to the cognitive bias of his own concept-oriented Christian background. In reviewing certain as yet unexplored common themes in Buddhism and Wieman, such as the emphasis on the impermanence and what Wieman calls "the dark realities of life," David Lee Miller stresses what is perhaps the closest resemblance—the way both link deep sensitivity to humanity's suffering with a type of philosophical analysis pursued in a uniquely Buddhist way. "Wieman," Miller writes, "is creating a tradition beyond all traditions, a tradition of creativity that calls us continually to the source of the good we experience in the momentary now. Wieman is thus working out a tradition without a distinct and adequate name." It is, Miller argues, a tradition calling attention to the creative forces, integrations, concrescences, and prehensions that synthesize reality everywhere on earth: "Persons are vivid centers of experience related each with one another and all other things in and on the earth, and we inherit and create along countless avenues of interchange. This is the shared perspective of Wieman and Buddhism, a perspective of free, full, and rich organic relatedness, as yet only slightly discerned and acted on within the pervasive, pulsating, moving centers of process that hold the promise of freeing us progressively from our tradition-bound moorings that bind, defile, and impoverish everything and everyone alive."[30]

The Buddhist themes in Wieman's work were recognized no doubt by many Asians, but one Japanese professor carried on a correspondence with Wieman for seventeen years. Invited by this professor, Ichirō Hara, an English professor at Waseda University, to join a Tokyo Fellowship of Creativity, Wieman became a member in 1962. Through the years, Hara expressed his delight over Wieman's gradual move from an explicitly Christian orientation to formulations more universal in nature, focusing increasingly on the problem of suffering and on the experience of life's greatest good. It was the empirical method of inquiry in Wieman that loomed large in Professor Hara's thinking, a type of empiricism that draws on experience in a wider range than the monolithic and deterministic empiricism that had died with David Hume two centuries before.[31] "Nothing can transform men and women," Wieman writes,

> *unless it actually operates in human life. Therefore, in human life here and now, in the actual present processes of human existence, must be sought what diminishes the suffering and increases the good. Not in some structure of the total universe, and not in any Being beyond the universe and beyond all structures of existence can the answer to the religious question be found. Beliefs about the "meaning" and*

*character of the totality of all existence, beliefs about what governs the universe, beliefs about the final outcome of human history, all these are not only illusions; they are evasive devices which direct human concern away from the area where the causes and conditions of man's transformation must occur, namely in human life itself.*[32]

This is precisely the method of analysis and experiential probing in which Buddhism was launched twenty-five centuries before.

Wieman's empirical theology shares deeply with Buddhism a sharp focus on the concreteness of an individual's original spontaneous experience, realizing that in so far as the emphasis is here no one will seek his or her security and value in a metaphysical system of belief. The many creator gods of the Buddha's native India were eliminated in this way. No one can diminish the suffering and discover the cure by accepting a metaphysical view. Wieman was always seeking to free men and women from the blind emotional clinging to what they mean to have, what they have no intention of giving up, what the logic of their own traditional theologies sought to prove must never be relinquished. Wieman and Buddhism both purge the emotions of those compulsive drives that lie behind the unsatisfactoriness and dark realities of life.

One of the letters in the Hara-Wieman correspondence is of special interest. In a letter written in February 1960, Wieman points out six features of his thinking that were also in a book on Buddhism that Professor Hara had sent him some months before: (1) the reliance on rigorous daily practice of worshipful meditation; (2) the rejection of all supernaturalism and philosophies that look beyond time to find what is most real; (3) the belief in the inseparability of dualisms such as life and death and body and mind, all such dualisms being merged into a single unity that must be experienced, disciplined, and enjoyed; (4) the repudiation of all belief, knowledge, and words as essential parts of the ultimate source of security and value; (5) the dependence on the directness of communication, person-to-person, as suggested by the term Creative Interchange; and (6) the insistence on the need to cast off the ego, where ego means the cramped, crippled, confined self that has developed from influences working upon everyone from infancy on. For Wieman, an individual's egoless experiences are properly linked in community with others and the encompassing world. "These," Wieman writes, "are points of similarity between Buddhism and my own work."

Wieman comments regarding the encounter between Christian and non-Christian traditions that is now taking place. "What shall we do about it?" he asks. "One answer says: 'Defend our traditions.' A second answer says 'Mix the traditions.' Both of these I think are mistaken. The third answer I defend. When diverse traditions confront one another, the way of salvation is found not in any one of them and not in any eclectic selection from them, but by further inquiry made possible by these opposing traditions. Religious inquiry under such conditions may find a better answer to the religious question than resides in any of the traditions."[33] Wieman here reveals his commitment to the kind of free and open inquiry that is the heart of modern science, a commitment attached to no particular conclusion about the world, regardless of how ancient and widely supported it may be. Wieman was so articulate in debate that it was sometimes difficult to see that he was committed, not to any concept of God, despite the remarkable virtues he saw in his own, but to the kind of creative interchange that would correct the errors present in all beliefs. He had digested the writings of America's only internationally known philosopher of science, Charles Peirce, who writes, "The opinion which is fated to be ultimately agreed to by all who investigate, is what we mean by the truth, and the object represented in this opinion is the real."[34]

How rare this commitment was in the academic circles in which Wieman was involved, and how far he had left his explicit Christian upbringing behind, can be witnessed by comparing Wieman and his major adversary at the time, the German émigré Reinhold Niebuhr, a new biography of whom has just been published.[35] Students at Union Theological Seminary both intellectually and literally sat at Niebuhr's feet; he wrote columns in daily newspapers, as well as in the *New Republic* and *Nation*, and founded his own biweekly, *Christianity and Crisis*; his portrait and the story of his career dominated the twenty-fifth anniversary issue of *Time*. Niebuhr was the most powerful Christian theologian in America from the 1930s through the 1960s. The dramatic distance Wieman had traveled from the theology in which he was reared stands out in sharp relief when placed alongside the views of this leading Christian intellectual of the time. It was Niebuhr's nonempirical theology Wieman was deliberately trying to overcome. This intellectual combat with Niebuhr furnished much of the motivation of Wieman's Chicago years— 1926–1946.

What distinguishes Wieman's empirical approach is the way his method of religious inquiry is able to explain all of Niebuhr's confident appeals to Christ as the key to the meaning of history and to an eternity "standing over time and at the end of time, the ultimate source of power of all derived and dependent existence, the ground and source of the mere succession of natural events, and to the self-justifying power of divine grace which completes what men and women are unable to complete, giving individuals a new vantage point above history from which to view the conflicts in a new light."[36]

"The Christian Gospel," Niebuhr argues, "enters the world with the proclamation that in Christ both 'wisdom' and 'power' are available to man; which is to say that not only has the true meaning of life been disclosed but also that resources have been made available to fulfill that meaning." Furthermore, "Grace represents on the one hand the mercy and forgiveness of God by which He completes what man cannot complete and overcomes the sinful elements in all of man's achievements. Grace is the power of God over man. Grace is on the other hand the power of God in man; it represents an accession of resources, which man does not have of himself, enabling him to become what he truly ought to be."[37] In the view of Niebuhr, the conditions of historical existence lead men and women to look for a Christ to complete their irreconcilable conflicts and incompleteness, to provide the basis outside history upon which history depends and to which history points as the ultimate fulfillment and justification of the obscurities, the contradictions, and the sufferings on the human level of life. Without this key, human life is threatened forever with meaninglessness. Without something transcending human wisdom, history would go on forever with its rumors of ever more disastrous wars.

We see here the antipode to process thought in religion. "Any appeal," Whitehead writes, "to a reality outside nature—the Absolute, Brahma, The Order of Heaven, God—to which we may appeal for the removal of perplexity, constitutes the great refusal of rationality to assert its rights."[38] Wieman and Buddhism agree.

According to Niebuhr, Christ has done two things: (1) symbolized the divine nature of God in history through his sacrificial love on the Cross and (2) opened a new channel of power in which God can work upon the individual who accepts this revelation of God's love. The fact that this revelation of the nature of God went down in defeat amid the conflicting jealousies of historical interests is only what should have been expected. Had the Christ been successful in the clash of contending drives, Niebuhr believes, it would have been plain that here was but another clash of human rivalries of which history is replete. In the apparent defeat, the paradoxical love of God stands apart from the love of man. God's love can be revealed within history only by a disavowal of power.[39] For Niebuhr, "It is impossible to symbolize the divine goodness in history in any other way than by complete powerlessness, or rather by a consistent refusal to use power in the rivalries of history." Vicarious suffering, furthermore, is the final revelation of meaning in history: "To declare, as Jesus does, that the Messiah, the representative of God, must suffer, is to make vicarious suffering the final revelation of meaning in history. But it is the vicarious suffering of the representative of God, and not of some force in history, which finally clarifies the obscurities of history and discloses the sovereignty of God over history."[40]

All of this becomes the most intelligible interpretation of human experience only as an individual accepts Christ as a final revelation of God. To such, Christ becomes the basis for a satisfactory total explanation of life, a witness of the presence of the transcendent pull of eternity over time, the base outside history upon which our historical experience depends. To the rest, Christ is another example of miserable defeat in the clash of conflicting interests.

According to the two volumes of Niebuhr's widely read book *The Nature and Destiny of Man*, the culmination of his life work, the fear of death that he attributes to all people is also evidence of the presence of the eternal: "The positive indication of man's freedom transcending nature is mind comprehending the point in nature at which his own existence in nature ends; thereby proving that nature does not fully contain him. The fact that he fears extinction is a negative indication of a dimension in the human spirit transcending nature. The fear of death is thus the clearest embryonic expression of man's capacity as a creator of history."[41] Were it not for the present interim between the true disclosure of history's meaning and the fulfillment of that meaning, humankind would have no basis for discovering the significance of human life.[42]

Wieman's empirical theology accounts for all phenomena submitted by Niebuhr in entirely naturalistic ways, without what Hartshorne calls "the idolatry of the Eternal," and without falling into the logical fallacy of thinking that what is everlasting must be eternal. "The true significance of death," Wieman writes,

> *is that it makes creativity possible. Only if death is accepted with full recognition of its true meaning, can creativity triumph. Death must come if creative good is to triumph. Without death new generations could not arise, youth could not appear and break through the hardening crust of class stratification, institutional fixation, and rigid habit formation. Without death in the background, vivid awareness of the unique individual swiftly flowing and soon to fade would not be with us; nor would we discern the precious meaning of the swiftly flying years. Without death, we could never attain that comprehensive perspective of the individual's whole life which can be had only after the irrelevancies, trivialities, and inconsistencies of bodily existence have ended. Without death, the creativity of life would sink and disappear beneath the dull routine of conformity because there would not be the ever renewed participation of unique individuals and new beginnings.*[43]

The most profound of Wieman's several attempts to deal with the meaning of death is perhaps those lines just quoted, but in the "technical postscript" of *The Source of Human Good*—the last words of his most important book—he has another perspective:

*Frail and brief must be the life of an organism sufficiently sensitive and responsive to bring the world to qualitative abundance. When man becomes sufficiently mature to apprehend the deeper meanings, he begins to die. The glow of life is always a sunset glow. Every supreme fulfillment is swiftly transitory in love, beauty, wisdom; and none is so swift in waning as the supreme union of these three. It cannot be otherwise. Resources of appreciative consciousness are not sufficient to withstand the onslaughts of change, the evil impulses of the heart, and the wearing-down of continued effort. This is the tragedy of man and of creative power. History cannot lift this fate, but it can make the glow of swift decline cumulative through a succession of generations. History can give to all things mean and noble a voice to speak from out the past, bringing to the sensitive mind a love of earth and all things in it and the sky above. In this way it can endow the dying day of each generation with a splendor deepening through the ages.*[44]

Wieman's empirical theology not only accounts for Niebuhr's phenomena; there are perspectives and issues of great magnitude that Niebuhr's theology cannot address. It is a matter open to public investigation, for example, that whatever have been the individual fates of nations and cultural epochs, there has been a progressive growth of meaning and a widening of horizons as the universe becomes a more appreciable world. Whatever has been the fate of early empires, out of every period of spasmodic and faltering enrichment there has issued an ever-increasing community of minds; the world has become more rich with quality to a wider and growing community of humankind. All people's interests are rapidly coming to interpenetrate. In spite of epochs of threatened relapse into barbarism, such as in the brief years of the Hitler misanthropy, the larger scope of events shows a direction toward a world of more sensitive human organisms encompassing the globe.

The creation of this more appreciable world, according to Wieman's philosophy, is the work of that "event" of towering importance that he calls Creative Interchange, analyzed into the four events explored above. Far from being the invasion of the temporal by the eternal, this empirically verifiable transformation of human experience brings men and women new perspectives, creating the enlarged and vivified organism, causing the world to become wider in its range of possibility, and conveying this enlargement of participation into a deepening community of humankind. The creative interaction and growth of a world shared in this way has the same transcending effect as what Niebuhr calls "the pull of the transcendent in human life." In Wieman this pull of the transcendent is seen in a new, empirical, more concretely evidential light.

No one, moreover, needs the witness of Niebuhr's transcendent Christ in order to live the crucified life; it is not only being lived every day by millions who have never heard of Christ, it is also the unavoidable experience wherever the compulsive grip of conscious and unconscious attachments is canceling out the spontaneous individualized experiences that constitute the ground floor of the human world. To direct attention away from this crucified living to the final culmination of history in Christ is to bring, among other things, nuclear destruction nearer than it already is. To increase the number of people who believe that they would meet Christ in such an end of the world is to increase partisans of the bomb, whatever they may say to the contrary. Belief in such an afterlife at this moment in history adds to the hazard of our time.

One of the major aims of Wieman's career was to foster "a new reformation of religion in relation to science," as he put it in a new journal devoted to that goal. "How can religion and science be united," he asks, "to make human existence at all levels more fit for the effective operation of that creativity which expands indefinitely the valuing consciousness of each individual in community with others to include all the diverse goal-seeking activities of human existence insofar as they can be brought into relations of mutual support?"[45] The empirical theology of Wieman is the commencement of a new seriousness in using the resources in the human sciences to work on the problem of identifying more precisely the process that sustains and vivifies the original experience of men and women in creative communication with others. The scientific enterprise for Wieman is relative to time, culture, and human purpose. What form either religion or science will take in the future we cannot know.[46]

## Dewey's Concept of God

In many ways the effort of Wieman to create a theology within the limits of experience found its strongest support in John Dewey. It was Dewey, according to Wieman, who led him to see that his philosophical theology must be directed to what actually and observably operates in human life.[47] Wieman admired Dewey for a living faith that runs deeper than words, and for perceiving that creative communication is more important than anything else in the world.[48] Wieman was as eager as Dewey to condemn all forces standing across the path of empirical inquiry in religion, but it was Dewey who saw, *perhaps for the first time in Western civilization*, that a commitment to *inquiry* could become so much a part of life that it takes on the central features of a religious life, generating a world more shareable, more knowable, more rich with qualitative meaning. His conviction grew that "whatever introduces genuine perspective is religious."[49]

The commitment to the self-corrective inquiry Dewey has in mind is another manifestation of love, and it is in this framework that Dewey offered in his Terry Lectures at Yale definitions both of religious faith and of God. We are each of us confronted, according to Dewey, with one of the ways of the world that calls for our devotion, a commitment and devotion that conserves, transmits, rectifies, and expands the "natural knowledge" that each generation endows upon the next:

*We who now live are parts of a humanity that extends into the remote past. The things in civilization we most prize are not of ourselves. They exist by grace of the doings and sufferings of the continuous human community in which we are a link. Ours is the responsibility for transmitting the heritage of values we have received that those who come after us may receive it more solid and secure, more widely accessible and more generously shared than we have received it. Here are all the elements for a religious faith that shall not be confined to sect, class, or race. Such a faith has always been implicitly the common faith of mankind. It remains to make it explicit and militant.*[50]

Dewey's definition of God points straight to the basic fact that sustains all hope in the face of an unpredictable future—the fact that our transactions with the world do not and need not remain *opaque*. The aspiration for natural knowledge leads to a more intelligible world. Caught without understanding in the face of situations that would submerge us, we all know the importance of an emerging meaning that joins actualities and idealities together, generating the "genuine perspective" Dewey thinks of as religious.

The *active* relation between the actual and the ideal is Dewey's definition of God. God is the mystery of those emerging meanings and perspectives of which there are never enough to make all our ends meet. God is *where* meanings emerge. God *is* wherever things are beginning to make sense. This, for Dewey, is the focus of religious faith, the faith by which he lived. God so defined was the deepening reality of all religions that have a "spiritual content."

Out of his pragmatic bent, for which he is too exclusively famous, Dewey says that such a perspective of the religious quest "seems . . . urgently needed at the present time" but that "men and women have never fully used the powers they possess to advance the good in life, because they have waited upon some power external to themselves and to nature to do the work they are responsible for doing. Dependence upon an external power is the counterpart of surrender of human endeavor. Nor is emphasis on exercising our own powers for good an egoistical or a sentimentally optimistic recourse. It is not the first, for it does not isolate man, either individually or collectively, from nature. It is not the second, because it makes no assumption beyond that of the need and responsibility for human endeavor."[51]

Dewey's formulation of what he called the search for "natural knowledge" is something to which he returned again and again throughout his career. For reasons I have indicated, this formulation is Dewey's greatest contribution to the rapidly developing need to "make more explicit and militant" our responsibility for transmitting to posterity a more shareable celebration of the wonder of being alive. It is Dewey's tribute to the creative interchange that is forever widening and deepening the community of values between individuals and peoples. Unless this interchange be characterized by the spirit of inquiry and self-correction, there is bound to be, as J. N. Findlay says in his Gifford Lectures, "violence in the whole attempt to make of our shared rational life the religious absolute many have attempted to make of it."[52]

## *"Toward a Buddhisto-Christian Religion"*

Unlike other process philosophers and theologians, who have been known to admit that the world in the concreteness of the present individualized experience is not the world their systematic theories describe,[53] Hartshorne agrees with Heraclitus that the world one thinks is the world one sees and acts in, shareable but not borrowed from others. More than other process philosophers, Hartshorne has heeded Bergson's warning regarding the tension between what is directly given in immediate experience and the abstract constructions of reason and science. He is also closer than other process philosophers to Buddhism.

The only leading Western philosopher to have studied Buddhism for almost a half century, Hartshorne praises Buddhism for returning us to an honest empiricism in which the concrete subjects are the momentary actualities, the individualized, self-creative, spontaneous experiences that ground the living world. He was prepared as a Harvard student to remember throughout his career the point Victor Lowe recollects their mentor, Alfred North Whitehead, making: "My occasion of experience is my present experience of the whole universe, and this status of individual experience is something no thinker can escape."[54] Like Whitehead, Hartshorne has always had this vivid appreciation of the immediacy of all value in the passing now. For both philosophers these "occasions of experience" are and remain forever, in Whitehead's words, "the really real things which in their collective unity compose the evolving universe, ever plunging into the creative advance." Whitehead states, "We experience the universe, and we analyze in our consciousness a minute selection of its details."[55]

Hartshorne is one of the major philosophers in the history of Western thought precisely because of his naked life-oriented empiricism, which argues that "enduring substances in a living world constitute an elemental confusion contrary to both logic and life, a fact taken into account by countless Buddhists for two thousand years, some of whom at least were constructive metaphysicians." As Lowe says, an empiricism that begins with Whitehead's actual entities — Lowe could as easily be speaking of Hartshorne's concrete momentary realities or Buddhism's self-active egoless nows — is an empiricism "that runs in the veins of all of us as a common bond."[56] Speaking out of such empiricism with enviable intellectual clarity, Hartshorne repeatedly affirms that concrete feelings and events, together with their creative novel interrelatedness, are all that is. Passing from one richly concrete actuality to another in "the creative synthesis that explains everything, including itself," these "fulfilled nows" need no more ultimate ground. "To have seen this so long ago," Hartshorne writes, "is the glory of Buddhism."[57]

Throughout the past two thousand years of Western civilization, however, the worship of infinite, immutable, absolute Being has been for most men and women an exercise in idolatry, with all the crippling side effects of alienation and violence to which Findlay refers. This worship is the major disputed point between Hartshorne and Wieman, whose transformation of Christianity, though it led to an invitation to join a group of Buddhists in Tokyo's Fellowship of Creativity, was, in Hartshorne's view, impaled on Wieman's concept of God. From the very beginning, Wieman presents a God who is superhuman in the sense of being "a source of human good," an identifiable event (actually four events) that transforms men and women as they cannot transform themselves. Creative Interchange is considered the divine event; the role of the human creature is to deal with what God has caused to emerge in their interchange and to provide conditions supportive of the divine creativity. To the end of his life Wieman continued to view "the event" in this way, seeing creativity in individual people as God's work, not theirs. For Hartshorne, on the other hand, God assumes the properties of a creativity beyond the insights of all religious traditions, with no determinate actuality but a presence in the infinite productivity of new actualities; God is the model of the creativity that sustains the universe. As he remarked in an interview with William S. Minor in New York in 1976, "Wieman's argument that Creative Interchange must be considered superhuman cannot get started in my philosophy. As Bergson puts it, 'Every man is an artist creating each moment his own experience.' Jules Lequier said it a hundred years before: 'God has created me creator of myself.' The ultimate function of God is to enable life in the world to add up to something."[58] Creative Interchange, in Hartshorne's view, is how creatures act from the vital center of things; it is not the God they serve.

Hartshorne's view of God as the model of creativity is reminiscent of the Buddhist concept of the interrelatedness of things — "creative origination," "conditioned genesis," or *pratītya-samutpāda*, all of which are synonyms of *śūnyatā*. Unless translations entirely misconstrue the original intent, *śūnyatā* has never been either the Oneness in which everything and everyone culminate in a Supreme Identity or the Oneness in which everything and everyone lose their identity forever in some vast cosmic evacuation. Either of these alternatives would overlook the constant struggle Buddhism has maintained to preserve the openness, the freedom, the nonattachment, and the continuity implied in its concept of relational origination.

In the Hartshornean-Buddhist view creativity never ceases. There is a new Many in every momentary emerging One. What makes it possible to speak of the Buddhist nirvana is that all acquisitive feelings attached to previous moments can be eliminated in the richness of the present moment. The *now* is forever; the fleeting instant is preserved in the vast interrelatedness of existence. This is why Inada can say that "for the Buddhist, he who embodies *śūnyatā* by attaining Enlightenment lives forevermore." As Whitehead puts it, "The immediate facts of present action pass into permanent significance for the universe."[59] These momentary nows, each an aesthetic fact of life, are identifiable to the extent that men and women awaken and become aware, and learn to cherish them in memory and perception with compassion for these living centers of a self-creative world. Each one is part of the inheritance of the past, differing from one another chiefly in the scope and range of their participation in a vast social process, no element of which is determined in advance.

The significance of the passing moment is not only found in its self-enjoyment and self-creativity, but also in what it contributes to something more enduring than itself and its immediate matrix; its ultimate significance is measured by its contribution to the self-surpassing oneness of the world where nothing and no one is ever either destroyed or forgotten, where everything and everyone has made a difference forevermore. In both Hartshorne and Buddhism, this is what gives aim and purpose to human life. "The aesthetic value of life," Hartshorne writes, "is realized in relation to other individuals *and* to the cosmos; its eventual worth will come in the contribution it has made to something more enduring than any animal or species," all of whom will eventually give way to something still beneath the horizons of the world.[60]

"To be entirely rational," Hartshorne continues, "is to love the whole ongoing universe, overcoming self-centeredness, and to feel oneself and one's future as items in that universe—for that is to see things as they are." For Hartshorne, this rationality is opposed to self-concern. Indeed, "not even sub-rational animals in fact derive their other-regarding behaviour from self-concern. The notion that self-preservation is the law of nature is poor biology. Species-preservation is closer to the true law." As Hartshorne says, "The basic motivation is neither the appeal of a self for that same self; nor even the appeal of other selves for the own self. Rather, it is something more general and yet, in its instances, more specific or concrete—the appeal of life for life. . . . Apparently it was Buddha who discovered this, centuries before Christ, if I may so speak, rediscovered it."[61]

Because of the alienation inherent in all linguistic systems, Hartshorne has had moments when he was tempted to agree with Buddhism that efforts to heighten awareness of the "creative synthesis that explains everything, including itself," are not helped by attempting to formulate this ultimate ground in theistic terms.[62] In the essay of 1984 from which the title of the present section is taken, he confesses to having been "one-sided," emphasizing the theoretical at the expense of what he calls "the nonconceptual, nontheoretical apprehension of reality," to having written "as though the merit of Buddhism was that it had the right theory of the self and of motivation, but that what we need is a still better theory." Hartshorne believes, however, that we need more than any theory: "We even need a certain freedom from theory (insofar as Nāgārjuna's criticisms of conceptual under-standing are justified). Self-interest and substance theories are hampering, they imprison us, but life at its best is no mere appli-cation of theory, however good. We have to respond to situations always more complex than we can understand, and we have to respond with more than understanding. We need to feel as well as think in good ways. We need to be artists in living, creative as well as kindly. Buddhist meditation has this as its purpose."[63] The following year Hartshorne, after reading the manuscript of my *Understanding Buddhism* recognized the Buddhist view as closest and the "strongest rival" to his own. As a letter written at the time states, "If I ask myself, 'What view might be right if yours were wrong?' I find myself answering, 'The Buddhist view as Jacobson presents it.' "[64]

In a letter written the same day he, however, speaks more in the spirit of the West, stating what he considers the main distinction between Buddhism and himself—a greater stress upon the role of concepts (over against meditation) in penetrating the aesthetic process of qualitative enrichment or "pure experience" that char-acterizes the experiences of everyday life: "If I felt I had to give up my side in this difference, my second guess would be your more Buddhist view; for the present, however, I think that concepts in general, and the concept of deity as summing up all the meta-physical concepts, go deeper and are less dispensable than your view takes them to be."[65] When one remembers that language is part of the web of life, as Henry Stapp has put it, and that in a changing world concepts can be improved only by opening them to persisting probing and criticism, as Hartshorne has himself insisted throughout his long career, it remains questionable whether any concept of the divine can entirely avoid the atmo-sphere of absurdity while seeking to express the limitlessness of human experience within the limits of language. Any concept of the divine can deepen and vivify the balanced intensities of expe-rience only in the solitariness of an individualized existence. This is what both Hartshorne and Buddhism (with Nāgārjuna, for example) have always contended. But here, too, Hartshorne may be "more Buddhist than some Buddhists," as he has suggested, in suspecting that "the renunciation of metaphysical concepts as such suits the need of many individuals but not of all."[66]

The present century heralds a new willingness on the part of some theologians in the West to overcome the most egregious flaws in their ancient tradition. These Western theologians have been struggling, for the first time with utmost seriousness, against the stereotyped symbols of their tradition in order to provide for men and women a more plausible perspective from within their own individualized experience in the world. New theological discoveries are being communicated from within the vastly deepened and extended awareness of people who are now members of a community that embraces all the subcultures of the earth. In one of the breakthroughs of Western thinking, deities that have symbolized ego-centeredness and provincialism at their worst have been put out to pasture along with their counterparts from an even more ancient past. For a hundred years a new type of theologian has been returning individuals from the high abstractions of conscious thought and from the cultural stereotyping of their individualized life in the world, offering new alternative ways of being at home. In the present century, Marjorie Grene writes, the most profound and comprehensive effort of this sort has been the philosophy of Whitehead.[67] And theology in Hartshorne has become an effort of rationality to express a knowledge that is likewise love, and to communicate the rich fullness of those aesthetic foundations of the world that return men and women from the institutionalization of their lives, from the abstractness, the lack of closeness to life in the momentary now. The teachings of the Buddha, spoken in the framework of a radically different culture, reflect the same practical and eminently rational concern.

The present century also heralds the end of the ability of a linguistically encapsulated culture to define the horizons within which men and women will reflect upon the source of meaning and value. From this historically unprecedented point forward none of the self-encapsulated cultures of the human community will be able with complete plausibility to think theologically for the whole world. An infinitely rich and evolving universe with novelty built into its all-embracing oneness brings before the bar of critical opinion everything that has been said, pro and con, about God. Theology henceforth will pursue its distinctive insights from within the vastness of experience itself.

# 6. The Religion of Analysis and the Spirit of Modern Science

*The glory of the nineteenth century has been its science. It was my ines-
timable privilege to have felt as a boy the warmth of the steadily burn-
ing enthusiasm of the scientific generation of Darwin, most of the leaders
of which at home I knew intimately, and some very well in almost every
country of Europe. The word* science *was one often in those men's
mouths, and I am quite sure they did not mean by it "systematized
knowledge," as former ages had defined it, nor anything set down in a
book, but, on the contrary, a mode of life; not knowledge, but the
devoted, well-considered life-pursuit of knowledge; devotion to the truth
that the man is not yet able to see but is striving to obtain. The word
was thus, from the etymological point of view, already a misnomer. And
so it remains with the scientists of to-day.*

Charles Sanders Peirce, The Nineteenth Century

*The great scientific contribution in theoretical physics that has come
from Japan since the last war may be an indication that it is easier to
adapt oneself to the quantum-theoretical concept of reality when one
has not had to free oneself from the naive materialistic way of thinking
that still prevailed in Europe in the first decades of this century.*

Werner Heisenberg,
Physics and Philosophy: The Revolution of Modern Science

The movement of modern science from the fringes of life to the
vital center constitutes one of the great transition points in
human history, comparable to the transition from precivilization
to civilization in the upper reaches of the Fertile Crescent ten

thousand years ago. The most powerful social process shaping the daily lives of everyone on the planet is scientific research. It is disentangling people from the rigidity and inflexibility that constitute their most intimate bond with death. It is teaching them for the first time to use their minds, not to seek reassurance in the face of life's suffering and anxiety and not to look for some escape from the transitoriness that is one of the fundamental features of existence, but to strengthen and multiply the connective links that establish human life more firmly in its natural habitat, rendering more transparent our relations with one another and with the speechless world's fellow-creatures. It is the life-style, therefore, that now has the highest survival value.

This is the condition, never encountered in the past, that confronts all the great civilizations of the modern world. In order to maintain their relative position and power, these civilizations must embrace scientific research as their major industry and new information as their major resource; this information in turn inundates old distinctions and modes of interpretation, along with a vast system of cultural levees and dams. No set of conceptual metaphors, however rich in novel possibilities of construal, can foresee and control the discoveries of science within the parameters of the social structures and value systems already in place. No area of human concern is altogether immune to the germ that is born when a truly deep scientific discovery is made. As Gunnar Myrdal argues, "Taking as given the civilization in which it takes place, the accelerating growth of scientific and technological knowledge becomes a force, speeding up and bending the course of history in a way that is largely outside our control." In such conditions, Whitehead writes, "the rule is absolute, the race which does not value trained intelligence is doomed. Not all your heroism, not all your social charm, not all your wit, not all your victories on land or at sea, can move back the finger of fate. Today we maintain ourselves. Tomorrow science will have moved forward yet one more step, and there will be no appeal from the judgment which will then be pronounced on the uneducated."[1]

The major function of modern science, it now seems clear, has been to liberate humankind from the conventional, parochial, custom-bound ways of the traditional culture-worlds in which it has been maturing for four centuries in the West. The British philosopher of science Sir Karl Popper remarks that "it is part of the greatness and the beauty of science that we can learn that the world is utterly different from what we ever imagined — until our imagination was fired by the refutation of our earlier theories. There does not seem any reason to think that this process will come to an end."[2] The long search in Western civilization for intellectual certitudes we shall never need to change is finally over. No permanence is attached to anything scientists say about the world; everything known is only provisionally true. "We cannot be sure," Peirce writes, "that the community will ever settle down to an unalterable conclusion about any given question. All that we are ever entitled to assume is in the form of a *hope* that such conclusion may be substantially reached concerning the particular questions with which our inquiries are busied."[3]

More and more the fate of every human community depends upon the willingness of individuals and groups to free themselves from the older methods of conceptual attachment and social conformity, freeing themselves to correct inflexible attitudes in themselves and others. In the long run this ability to rise above conflicts between old beliefs and new must become central if people are not to lose interest in their own relations to the world. The continuing screening of new knowledge forces upon us what one prominent scientist calls "the number one problem of our times, the need to shape up our value systems to something more in tune with present-day reality, more properly suited to the new powers that man now commands and the new problems we now face."[4] Viewed in this cultural perspective, science is not the newest cognitive feat in the long Western preoccupation with epistemological models. It is one of the central ways in which free creatures seek a more secure foothold in an uncertain world. Until now, no nation has ever educated its citizens to support the kind of reality testing, self-correction, and innovation that characterize modern science throughout the earth.

Any society from now on that fails to institutionalize scientific research and assimilate its methods of self-corrective behavior to all areas of life will lack the strength to resist a society that has done so. When the world is awash with the explosive power of new discovery, a community may easily destroy itself through attachment to obsolete and exhausted beliefs. In areas of health, crime, genetics, politics and other social sciences, and religion, the most powerful nation can commit collective suicide by remaining compulsively attached to ideas that have had their day.

The race is on, therefore, for every nation to increase the percentage of its population whose imaginative powers are free to structure reality in novel ways, who can imagine how data might be viewed in ways contrary to prevailing thought, and who possess capacities needed throughout the planet for a renewed confidence in the creativity everywhere in evidence in the growth of new knowledge. According to Ilya Prigogine, every modern society needs now to embrace "the new scientific revolution in which, in a period not unlike the birth of the scientific approach in ancient Greece or of its renaissance in the time of Galileo, the very position and meaning of science are undergoing reappraisal."[5]

More and more the fate of the species depends upon the willingness of individuals and groups to correct all their judgments, whether about themselves and their adversaries, or about the rest of nature. Science must become so much a part of the modern nation that it lives in the cultural underground as something that is taken for granted by all. It is not enough for any modern nation to have only one per cent of its population aware that the classical model of nature has been shaken in its very foundations.[6] It is not sufficient that so few should be carrying the enormous responsibility of keeping their society abreast of new discoveries such as the breaking of the genetic code, the mapping of the human cell, the discovery of the plasmic state of matter, and other research forcing a community *in the end* to rethink everything hitherto known about the world.

Major nations are in this kind of competition with one another. Generations now alive will witness the downfall of nations in which science is effectively trapped, by institutions that become monuments to the ego-centered drives of the few, by a military-industrial complex powerful enough to turn research away from natural curiosity toward weapon systems, by culturewide habits to manipulate and exploit everything and everyone in sight in the achievement of preconceived, predetermined ends, and by the vast undercurrent of childish persuasion that civilization consists in the proliferation of human wants. In all of these respects, the greatest challenge confronted by the major nations of the West comes, not from their own exclusive membership, but from the heavily impacted Buddhist nation of modern Japan.

## Science Through the Buddhist Looking Glass

It may take a long time for the West to recognize that Japan has been and remains capable of creative achievements in modern science, though Joseph Needham's monumental research on science among the Chinese has helped to break the Western parochialism in its persuasion that wisdom was born among the Europeans.[7] The reversal in the relations between nations East and West has come too suddenly to be taken fully into account, particularly the shift in the main currents of the world's life to the Pacific Basin and the most populous nations on earth. This shift may, in fact, turn out to be as significant for Western civilization as the Renaissance, the Reformation, and the Scientific Revolution combined.

It was a culture shock of the first order when Werner Heisenberg told us a quarter century ago that "great contributions in theoretical physics had come from Japan since the last war" and that the reason for such contributions might properly be sought in the Buddhist concept of the organic wholeness of the world, the concept of *śūnyatā* and the interrelatedness of existence.[8] Unconsciously, any Japanese coming of age in this ancestral culture tends to see things, including him- or herself, as part of an unfragmented whole, in contrast to the Western dualistic perspectives that generate the spectator point of view, an essentially adversarial relation between the observer and the rest of nature. In a Buddhism-impacted culture the nonexistence of any such fragmentation between independent and separate substances is assumed.

Research by Tadanobu Tsunoda on the human brain shows that reason and emotion are characteristically interwoven in the left brain hemisphere of the normal Japanese who has been reared in the ancestral language.[9] Seizo Ohe concludes from the Tsunoda research that as long as the Japanese continue to use their language they will share both personalities and a culture-world intimately rooted in a feeling of closeness with one another and with the rest of nature.[10] "The Buddhist tradition which underlies Japanese mentality at all social levels," Professor Ohe writes, "has saved

modern Japan from the so-called 'science shock,' which afflicted
the Western world especially with the biological theory of evolution in the 19th century. With their peculiar immunity to 'science
shock,' the Japanese people seem now particularly encouraged to
establish a plain common-sense attitude of looking at things as
they are revealed by science, and at the same time watching
science for its possible misuse from a human point of view. This
must be one of the most important features of the coming world
civilization of all mankind." Japan's leading philosopher of
science, Seizo Ohe looks forward to "a golden age of Japanese
science and technology to come in the near future for the benefit
of mankind."[11]

Chinese science for centuries prepared the Japanese for assimi-
lating the science of the West. In addition, such important discoveries as the heliocentric theory of Copernicus and Newton's
theory of gravitation came through the influence of the Dutch at
Nagasaki during the closing years of the eighteenth century. "By
the beginning of the 19th century," one study concludes, "a
knowledge of western science had been widely diffused among
the generality of the educated classes and the rich merchants."[12]
The Charter Oath of the Emperor Meiji carries the now famous
words "Knowledge shall be sought throughout the world," and
Japan's organic ties with China carried home the Confucian dic-
tum "Study as if life were too short and you were on the point of
missing it."[13] As Sorai Ogyū, writing at the turn of the eighteenth
century, expresses the orientation of Japan: "Learning consists in
widening one's information, absorbing extensively anything and
everything one comes upon."[14]

In a culture heavily impacted with Buddhism, though, science
has a different meaning than it has in the West. In the entire history of modern revolutionary discoveries, there has been no point
at which the traditions of Japan have been in conflict with contemporary scientific research. The "Japan Way" is to avoid the
separation of language from life and to keep from suffocating the
vividness and rhythm of experience in a flow of words. Forms of
understanding, including science, are viewed, therefore, as so
many possibilities for realization in a changing world; they are
probes to root out the fragmentary and routine confinements of
life. The Japanese, in fact, anticipated by several centuries the

Freudian understanding that conscious processes are not the major instruments for learning, real learning occurring on preconscious nonverbal levels. And they anticipated by many centuries the discovery of David Hume that intellect is rooted in feeling. They were less vulnerable, therefore, to Wittgenstein's warning against the bewitchment of the intellect by language—including the language of science.

It is the Buddhist background in Japanese culture that sustains the most persevering struggle among modern nations to keep from becoming enveloped, Gulliver-fashion, in those linguistic, ideological, political, and technological forms that reduce awareness to the limits of the tribe, social class, age level, and nation, and to the confinements of a particular time and place. Instead of acquiring the typically Western tendency, in Peirce's words, "to cling tenaciously, not merely to believing, but to believing just what we do believe,"[15] the Japanese come of age with a remarkable unconscious adjustment to uncertainty and doubt regarding the realities with which they have to deal.

With regard to one of the major obstacles, therefore, to open and revolutionary scientific discovery, the Buddhist-oriented Japanese have no place for individuals or groups who cannot change their minds and cannot open their minds to new information. The Japanese form a community in search of error sharply defined, with minds ready to criticize and investigate everything that is going on. Every aspect of the Japanese culture is constantly being subjected to a barrage of criticism coming from all walks of life. Public opinion polls express their restless drive for self-correction, and the aggressive quest for information has become one of the primary functions of government ministries and large industries in Japan, where people are sent out to bring back in-depth studies of every conceivable possibility or problem. In all areas of public and private interest—banking, health, education, industrial productivity, international trade, transportation, and world peace—public and private bureaucracies are operating as schoolmasters in a continuing campaign to disseminate and discuss information over a videoculture more than half of which is educational television.

In all of these respects, science has a wider and different meaning in a culture heavily impacted with Buddhist perspectives. As

Robert Guillain reports in *The Japanese Challenge*, Japan "is a whole nation that knows it is heading for the future, a whole society that is turned toward the coming years."[16] In some nations, people called "intellectuals" are held responsible for self-correction, but in Japan a society with deep fellow-feeling for one another is highly motivated for learning. Bookstores abound, and they are almost as crowded as the Tokyo Tower. The Japanese read more books and newspapers than any people on the planet. (As of 1979, each of the two largest newspapers had a circulation of over six million, four times the size of the largest in the United States.) There is, furthermore, a virtual absence of dropouts in the most demanding primary and secondary schools of the modern world. And Japanese youth, Ezra F. Vogel says, "substantially outperform their counterparts in modern Western nations, particularly in science and mathematics."[17] Children attend school six days each week for over forty weeks in order to meet government regulations, which require each school to operate an educational program for at least 240 days each year, compared to 180 days for the American school.[18]

With this background, it was a natural phenomenon that Jokichi Takamine first synthesized adrenalin (in 1901), that Hideyo Noguchi contributed to the pathology of yellow fever and syphilis, and that Hideki Yukawa won the Nobel Prize for predicting the meson in ways that led to later confirmation. Japanese science and industry, Seizo Ohe says, "are contributing daily to the creation of a world common to all men beyond races and cultures, helping to establish the philosophical and cultural foundations of the future world civilization mankind needs for its survival. Having experienced a bit of what a nuclear war can be in the future, Japan has a world-historical mission to prevent such a war by all means, from whatever ideological camp it may flare up."[19]

In a culture-world rooted in the Buddhist self-corrective outlook on life, the output of science covers the entire spectrum of human concerns, and not only such matters as Heisenberg's "quantum-theoretical concept of reality." No one can write a history of science in the culture-world of Japan, therefore, without preparing for the task with a deep grounding in the self-corrective Buddhist Way, because Japan's rise to leadership in modern science must be seen as a natural expression of its citizens' typically Buddhist freedom from thought attachment and compulsive believing, both of which have been major features of Western civilization for at least two thousand years. Science in the West has had to fight such intellectual clinging every step of the way, and many of the conclusions of scientific research have been transmuted into instruments of social control as soon as they were discovered. In Japan, however, the flow of information has become more powerful than conventional abstractions. Because Buddhism over the centuries has become so thoroughly suffused and blended with the cultural atmosphere that it is no longer differentiated as such, science as self-corrective living has become a style of life.

As long as Western parochialism continues in force, nothing will seem more surpassing strange than the way Japan's Buddhist "Looking Glass World" has prepared these inhabitants of the northern islands to move beyond their own explicit upbringing into the unpredictable consequences of total involvement with the modern world. An island-bound people, culturally at the end of the line of communication with people of the Eurasian continent, with no one to whom they could transmit whatever had come to them out of Indian and Chinese beginnings, they responded in a manner contrary to even their own expectations. Instead of becoming ingrown and insular in the fashion of the nations from whom they had learned the most, the Japanese have become the most fully self-corrective and outgoing creatures on the face of the earth, leading the contemporary world in the unitary interchange and community of learning that now envelops the globe. Their terminal position in receiving cultural transmissions from the rest of Asia and the West now serves as a launching pad for the twentieth century's rediscovery of humanity's most essential truth, that everything is connected and can communicate freely with everything else, thus transcending all linguistic, ancestral, racial, historical, religious, and national bounds.

Cultures with a decisive Buddhist component have no conflict between science and religion. In such cultures, science and religion provide, on the contrary, considerable harmonious mutual support. As a Thai professor and member of the American Philosophical Association writes: "In the history of Buddhism, there have been no disputes between religious beliefs and scientific knowledge, since Buddhism at no point comes into conflict with science. Albert Einstein held the same opinion: 'If there is any religion that would cope with modern scientific needs it would be Buddhism.' Buddhism does not ask its followers to believe in anything outside the normal order of nature."[20] And a professor of religious studies with extensive field work in East Asia writes that "while Christianity has waged a running battle with science in the years since Darwin, Buddhism has, in recent years, gained mounting recognition as the religion or philosophy most compatible with scientific methods and conclusions; in the statistical nature of physical 'laws' we can see parallels to Buddhism's views of the universe as changing, relative, interrelated, participatory."[21]

The most important major element Buddhism and modern science have in common is their central character of being self-corrective. This is the theme of a chapter in my own *Buddhism and the Contemporary World*, in which I discuss, among others, Nyanaponika Mahathera, an internationally known Buddhist from Sri Lanka, and Charles Hartshorne, a leading American philosopher, both of whom consider Buddhism and modern science the two self-corrective communities in the world.[22] Both Buddhism and modern science have labored in their own cultural matrices for centuries to induce humanity to accept the transitoriness of relations and events. Both are threatened with extinction among inflexible people, people who are forever looking for evidence to support what they already know. Both are forever seeking new insight, more enlightened views.

Buddhism, however, has one advantage over modern science as practiced in the West—its methods of meditation, which enable individuals to regain control over automatic mechanisms of habit and compulsive drives that otherwise rule behind our backs. Meditation practiced daily helps an individual to correct the nursery, counteract the power of the glands, modify the distortions acquired in the coming of age, and become more attentive and aware of what is actually going on. Methods of meditation are designed to counteract the subtle conditioning of self-centered and obsolete cultural systems, freeing life in its social dimensions to work for peace in a world boiling from time to time in tendencies toward nuclear destruction. If this meditative discipline becomes part of the education of scientists everywhere, it will become a factor in freeing creative resources for a more fully self-corrective life, because the only science humanity can with confidence support at this crucial juncture in civilization is one that is corrigible and creative in an all-sided, unparochial way. What scientists will find on close acquaintance with Buddhism is a discipline to create capacities for standing unfalsified and whole, a discipline that frees personal resources to operate without suppression and distortion. Imaginative powers will then be free to structure reality in novel ways, ways contrary to prevailing opinion. These are the qualities we need in reviving throughout the planet a renewed confidence in creation.

# 7. The Civilization of Experience

*Mankind is distinguished from animal life by its emphasis on abstractions. The degeneracy of mankind is distinguished from its uprise by the dominance of chill abstractions, divorced from aesthetic content.*

Alfred North Whitehead, Modes of Thought

*The one quest is an experience of self-acceptance, where "self" does not stand for a preconceived notion or image but is the experiential self-reality moment after moment. Above all, it is an experience of experiencing. For this is what consciousness means, what openness means, what surrendering leads into, what remains after the veils of conditioned perception are raised, and what the aim of acceptance is.*

Claudio Naranjo, The One Quest

The supreme aesthetic achievement of the twentieth century and the act with the greatest political fallout may well prove to be the launching of citizens of the earth into outer space. Freed from the gravitational field of the planet, these space travelers have seen the history of their species floating like a beautiful agate in a sea of darkness, the blue oceans of their homeland and the grey contours of land discernible from time to time in the rays of the sun. For a few moments they have stood free from the established order in which they were reared, stood where everything of purely local significance is flooded with the reality and the wonder of the good earth. Almost all of these men and women have stated publicly that strange new perceptions such as the earth rising on the horizon of the moon changed their thinking forever with respect to their individualized experience of the world.

Through television coverage millions of people have accompanied their fellow citizens in their giant steps for humankind. Many have felt their environment vastly enlarged, old limits pushed outward by new perception. Many have been moved by a new sense of urgency lest the problems of civilization below endanger the wonder-inspiring matrix of life. For many the new perception has become a new point of departure for exploring the possibilities of a civilization as generous toward the phenomenon of life as the earth itself.

The unprecedented perspective from beyond the pull of gravitational systems will be retained in the memory of the species forever, and it will continue to change the way millions of men and women think about their relations with the undivided environment that for a moment was totally there. On the horizon of their awareness they have become members of more than a million earth-bound species of animals, tens of thousands of them vertebrates, all nestled in one or another of the crossroads of nature, and all responsive to a niche prepared and preserved for them for millions and millions of years.

The political and cultural fallout of this aesthetic achievement of science and technology has created a collision with the way men and women have hitherto thought about their experience in the world. The memory of the beautiful earth floating as a life-supportive system in a sea of darkness points us to the deepest polar contradiction in the contemporary world—five billion people are born with the capacities for living in radically different linguistic and cultural systems, yet all of them are fixated, attached, and emotionally and intellectually bound by one system from the cradle to the grave. Many, however, have perceived the need to break the compulsive grip of their self-centered and parochial ways and adopt species-centered and life-centered views. Many have felt the need to think from the perspective of human experience and life, rather than from the viewpoint of a particular nation or social class. Our citizens in outer space have dramatized what Edward T. Hall calls "the journey beyond culture which breaks the cultural bind."[1]

No great civilization will ever again be permitted to behave as though it were the only one; each must be open to the scrutiny of all the others, lest the biosphere be endangered by radioactive wastes and acid rain, or by destruction of the ozone layer protecting all people from intolerable amounts of ultraviolet rays of the sun, or by nuclear weapons accumulating in mounting stockpiles under the control of people who think in the culture-bound patterns of the past. As Robin Fox writes: "In the past, it has not mattered greatly what people believed about themselves and their societies, since nothing that followed from these beliefs could have endangered the species. Within the next fifty years or even less, however, men and women must move to a *species-centered* view of the human world, taking their survival consciously into account, or they may not survive as a species. This requires a revolution in thinking as serious as the Copernican revolution half a millennium ago."[2]

Over a century ago Nietzsche locked himself into the same problem; everything he wrote turned around the problem of civilization: What is it? How has it been achieved? How can it be preserved?[3] In one of his notebooks from the 1870s, Nietzsche writes: "If mankind is not to destroy itself, there must be discovered as a scientific criterion for ecumenical goals, *a knowledge of the conditions of culture* which surpasses all previous levels of knowledge. Herein lies the immense task for the great minds of the next century."[4] But what are the current conditions for cultural renewal, now that Nietzsche's "next century" has passed?

## The Problem of Civilization

Awareness of the problem of civilization has vastly increased in recent years. Like our self-awareness in regard to dread diseases, this appreciation and self-appraisal as a civilization appears to be growing by leaps and bounds. No earlier civilization ever became alert to the presence of decay as quickly as has our own. Rome slept on for two or three centuries after the initial steps toward her own decline had been taken, and she simply could not see until almost the brink of her demise the oncoming avalanche of defeat; she considered herself eternal. Policies eventually adopted to stem the tide of Rome's disintegration present the sympathetic reader with a dramatic spectacle in which the best minds of the day were applying patches in the dark. Our own civilization, on the other hand, despite the faster pace at which events now sweep forward, is all about us becoming alert to the threat of self-destruction. This alertness is by no means traceable entirely to the launching of our citizens into outer space, nor to the ominous threat of nuclear bombs, since studies in economic history and in-depth studies of mental and emotional disorders were already spreading among the reading public the sense that the very premises of civilized life were under serious threat. This growing alertness has been submerged only briefly and superficially ever since. It is entirely possible that ours may become the first civilization to make the discovery that enables the civilizing process to avoid the precipice that has lain athwart the path of the great civilizations of the world.

It is essential at the outset to determine what the word *civilization* means. The word has been used in a variety of ways, seldom with precision and rarely in ways that elicit broad response, ever since it became current in the middle of the eighteenth century. It has been used rather loosely to refer to any social organization or to a growth of arts and sciences, or it has been counterposed to barbarism without further definition. Some definitions consist entirely of metaphor. For Spengler, for example, civilizations are organic unities, not otherwise specified, successively passing through the greening shoots of spring, the vigorous warmth of creative summer, the maturity of autumnal wisdom, and the cold gloom of a disintegrative winter. The word is used by Toynbee, on the other hand, as a methodological device, each civilization being "the smallest unit of historical study at which one arrives when one tries to understand the history of one's own country: the United States, say, or the United Kingdom."[5] Western civilization is such a unitary stream. Built out of a million imperceptible microdetails, its main core includes a life-stream of tools beginning in Asia Minor ten thousand years ago and a legacy of Greek thinking, the Christian religion, the Renaissance, the Protestant Reformation and subsequent Counter-Reformation, the French Revolution, the scientific revolution, the commercial and industrial revolutions, and the communist and democratic revolutions in Russia and the North Atlantic nations. (Though geographically in the Western Hemisphere, Latin American nations are not part of the life-stream of Western civilization, having missed several features of the common core.) Such items as Picasso's art, the poetry of William Butler Yeats, and the war in Vietnam can be understood only in the framework of Western civilization so defined.

Philosophers have tried, furthermore, to establish the "essence" of civilization in humanity's mental life, Hegel going so far as to equate the unfolding of the Absolute Idea with the process of civilization. Other students, Rostovtzeff, in his lifelong study of Rome, for example, have found the locus of civilization in a social class: "Is it possible to extend a higher civilization," he asks, "to the lower classes without debasing its standard and diluting its quality to the vanishing point? Is not every civilization bound to decay as soon as it begins to penetrate the masses?"[6] Nietzsche also found the creative sources of civilization in a social class; but, he says, "the lower classes of unlearned men are our only hope. The learned and cultivated classes must be abandoned, and along with them, the priests, who understand only these classes and are themselves members of them. The greatest danger is the contamination of the unlearned classes by the yeast of modern education."[7] This focus on social class was the conclusion of Marx as well, as I have indicated in chapter 3: only the struggles of an entire social class can be expected to conquer the thingification and alienation of human labor and return civilization to its creative sources.

It is obvious from these few samples of multiple modes of understanding civilization that poverty, alienation, despair, crime, escapism, nihilism, and war will go on and on until the generic problem of civilization can be defined and located. It is also obvious that all of these specific problems are but symptoms of some kind of underlying disease, or failure to diagnose the source of the disorder. Are we prepared to concede that civilization is this sort of curse to humanity, that it constitutes in a great variety of forms the limit situation in the development of the species? Is civilization analogous to the dinosaur's unwieldy size and thick insensitive hide? Has the time returned for glorifying the noble savage? Is civilization some kind of ultimate diabolic dream with-

out roots in what is really real? Or, can we perceive one underlying source of all the cruelties of civilization, under whatever
sun, constitution, racial inheritance, class alignment, ethical
code, or cultural peculiarity?

## The Buddhist Solution

From a Buddhist point of view, civilization is a response to the
interrelatedness of existence — *śūnyatā, paticca-samuppāda,* and
their synonyms, relational origination, conditioned genesis, emptiness, the void, creative origination, nothingness, and dependent
origination. To be, according to Buddhism, is to be related, to be
moved by the creativity incarnate in the passing moment. To the
measure that a person has not been corrupted with the disorders
of civilization, there is a feeling of being united with the living
world; the movement of history is within ourselves. Civilization
is the human response to the creativity that expands the diversity, range, and richness of the qualities accessible to the valuing
consciousness of humankind.

In the Buddhist perspective, the generic problem of civilization
is the problem of providing conditions that foster awareness of
the flow of quality in the inarticulate rhythm of life. Civilizations
are linguistic, symbolic, and cultural systems that depend for
their vitality and power upon the qualitative fullness individual
men and women experience in their most selfless moments of
everyday life. Indispensably relevant to the analysis of everything
that happens in the process of civilization, this qualitative flow in
the passing moment is the tenderness of life itself amid the sense-
less brutalities of this world. As Whitehead has put it for all Buddhists, "The worth of any social system depends on the value
experience it promotes among its individual members," and it is
on this ground that a civilization demonstrates its ability to
survive.[8]

The real enemy to the forms of civilization, therefore, are the
forms themselves, all of them elaborations of the assumption
that majestic institutions of public power in the form of bureaucracies, political and ecclesiastical hierarchies, or international

establishments such as a League of Nations or United Nations have a natural mandate to instruct and persuade men and women everywhere regarding the meaning of their experience in the world. All the forms of civilization up to the present have been based upon the assumption that people adjust best to the ambiguous demands of life by acquiring from human groups much wiser than themselves the principles according to which they should live. Accepting their reliance and trust in the superior power and wisdom of others, civilized men and women have turned their backs on their own firsthand and original experience in its preconscious unverbalized qualitative flow.

In the Buddhist perspective, the real enemy to human civilization is not the social rebel disgruntled with the hand he or she has been dealt; it is those towers of self-centered, self-justifying agencies of social organization that telegraph their disregard of life by alienating men and women from the aesthetic richness of experience in its individualized form. Civilizations find their proper role in fostering conditions enabling people to find their security, their identity, their sense of worth and social participation in the dynamic organic relatedness in which life's richness and reality consist. Kenneth Inada has explored, for example, some of the ways in which the American civilization has come in recent years to incorporate certain features of the Buddhist *śūnyatā*:

> The influx of emigrants from all over the world . . . is unprecedented, constantly adding to the experiential enrichment of America, one major result of which is to keep the American open and fresh and incorporative. In Dewey's sense, the days of the absolutely fixed ideas and institutions are over. From the Buddhist viewpoint, actions taking place in America have the character of approximating or simulating a śūnyatā-oriented experience. We cannot, of course, be too presumptive. But there are qualities, such as freedom, freshness, vividness, movement, rest, vision and value that are realizable only because of the "empty" [śūnyatā] nature in which plural elements are thrashed out, assimilated and embodied in the on-going process. The process, which is through and through pragmatic, is at the same time self-perpetuating.[9]

## The Long Buddhist Perspective

Throughout the long biological and cultural evolution of humankind, no change in the character of life has been more fundamental than the one now creating a new human frontier. The first great transformation of this proportion occurred in places like Kenya's Lake Turkana and the Great Rift Valley where Lucy, the oldest and most complete skeleton of any erect walking human ancestor uncovered in the sifting of fossilized bones, was found in 1977.[10] Three million years ago in the same area the earth's strangest creature was discovering how to transmit through cultural forms whatever he or she was learning from one generation to the next. Crude scrapers and choppers from an ancient stone-tool technology take us back at least two and one-half million years to where intimate nomadic social groups free from proprietary concerns were nurturing and foreshadowing the human form that was to come. "As millennium upon millennium passed by," Richard Leakey says, "our brains got a little bigger, our wits a little sharper, and—most important of all—our social and cultural fabric grew more elaborate and richly patterned until ten thousand years ago, when we stood at the threshold of a revolution that was to transform the world."[11]

This second great transformation arrived thirty thousand years ago in Africa—and much later in the Fertile Crescent—with agricultural and social discoveries that freed people from the widening range and diversity of experience now associated with civilization. People now alive who still live in ways antedating this threshold of civilization number fewer than three hundred thousand. Communication, cooperation, and reconstruction of the physical environment enabled the gene pool carrying the human future to create forms of language, technology, science, and social existence that have found their highest unfolding in the spectacular high-tech systems of the present day.

During our own closing decades of the twentieth century the second threshold in the evolution of the species—the threshold of civilization—is announcing the exhaustion of its patterns with a century of global wars in which 150 million have lost their lives, with drug addiction, mounting suicides, terrorism, and other forms of self-destruction. Having lived for millennia divided into clearly different histories, traditions, and racial and ethnic groups, the species cannot now survive the consequences of these divisions under drastically changed circumstances now prevailing on earth. "It is hard to summon much confidence," the British astronomer Fred Hoyle, writes "in a future extending more than a few decades. We are living today, not on the brink of social disaster, as we often tend to think, but actually *within* the disaster itself."[12] The German Holocaust, where eighty million people passively accepted the values given to them to believe (and thereby gave to the world a new cliché on what it means to be "a good German"), the Italian Fascist slaughter of Ethiopians with the tacit support of the reigning pope, and the napalm bombing of Tokyo's civilian population at the rate of 180,000 roasted alive in a single night—all lie like a blanket of guilt on the reflections of the contemporary world. These things were done by the most highly civilized nations. The forms of civilization that advanced the arts and sciences for ten thousand years have suddenly become the forms of death.

The ominous apocalyptic visions found everywhere in the writings of our time have a more positive and hopeful side never found in the daily news. Great transformations are sweeping wildly across the planet, making it next to impossible for any individual or community to keep abreast. A third new frontier is emerging with an environment radically different from those of the past. The hypnotic grip of ancient traditions is being broken. Men and women the world over are being freed from the unconscious grip of their parochial ways, compelled by the way conventional lives are becoming irrelevant and worse. The first generations are now alive who feel that their personal identity and sense of social belonging have been stifled and falsified by the sociological communities in which they were reared. Individuals and communities are multiplying that can no longer be controlled within the limits of any of the interpenetrating cultures on the planet. The incubators of thousands of self-regarding, self-defining, self-insulating culture-worlds are being broken in a maelstrom of global communication.

Nothing like this has happened in the long biological and cultural evolution of the species. Unreported by the omnipresent eyes of the media, a massive change is occurring in the very center of gravity of human existence, in the very ground, so to speak, of our experience in a volatile world. It is a shift away from established culture-worlds hitherto the sole legitimate sources of meaning and value, over to a kind of cross-cultural interchange that brings to the forefront the unconventionalized qualities of everyday life. Such is the power of this drive toward aesthetic worth (Whitehead has called it "the drive of the universe") that sociological communities such as the family and the state are being stripped of their once intimidating authority and power. The responsibility falls upon the individual to find his or her way into the interrelatedness and creativity of the process that has raised humanity from bestiality into civilization. Gone is the anthropological concept of culture as a structure of artifacts, mental habits, and symbolic behavior transmitted from one generation to the next, winding like the ancient labyrinth around its members with an existence and momentum of its own. A leading anthropologist tells us that "the greatest feat of all is when, *one individual after another*, we free ourselves from the grip of unconscious culture."[13]

The coming of what we have called the third human frontier was already perceived by Nietzsche. "The ancient claims," he says, "are coming undone." The encapsulated condition of civilizations is over; each civilization has clothed its members in ideological and theological assurances that theirs is the one authorized center of validity and worth, but the cultural osmosis fostered by global interchange has brought such claims to a natural end. The idea that human experience has *direct access* to the social nature of reality, apart from the intrusion of social institutions, and that it has a vividness and intensity that cannot without pathological consequences be ignored, is an idea whose time has come. The function of rational cultural systems henceforth will be to foster the qualitative richness of experience, to awaken and alert us to the aesthetic foundations of the world.

We face the task, as Whitehead puts it, "of providing for a universe that is without bounds, for a learning that is world-wide, and for an emotional life whose springs lie below conventionalities."[14] We face the task of opening the way for life to enjoy itself in its own individualized centers of experience, disregarding the question of whether these really real occasions of enjoyment occur in one historic community or another. As Yujiro Ikemi, of Kyushu University's School of Medicine, said at the 1977 meeting of the International College of Psychosomatic Medicine in Kyoto, "We must try to communicate with the innermost territory of our existence." In Buddhist terms, what both Whitehead and Yujiro Ikemi have said is that we face the challenge of diminishing the distance between the self-perpetuating process that is forever creating a new world—the process of *śūnyatā*—and a civilization of social creatures trying to figure out ways to become successfully interdependent on a global scale.

This Buddhist perspective on the relation between civilization and what is most real—the process and interrelatedness of *śūnyatā* —is almost the direct opposite of the view that civilization should amalgamate the mentality and morality of other cultures into a cosmopolitan mix in which new generations will come of age. Civilization will become more deeply rooted in *śūnyatā* only as individuals feel themselves suffocating from the parochial and provincial limits of the cultural kindergartens in which they have been reared. It will occur only in men and women whose enthusiasm for sharing the self-centered and artificial values of their contemporaries has come to an end. It will flourish only with the breaking of attachments in order to locate one's identity, and find one's fellow-creatures, in the fecundity, the strangeness, the beauty in the vivid flow of life itself.

The Buddhist solution to the problem of civilization is for each individual to live self-correctively in ultimate dependence upon the creativity operating in the original individualized experience of people everywhere in ways that bring forth the novel forms of togetherness without which human civilization would have come to an end long ago. Advancing levels of complexity and diversity in individuals and culture-worlds are supportable only by men and women who accept richness of quality as the great good of life. Whoever would participate in the new levels of advanced civilization must break the compulsive unconscious grip of their noblest ideals and stay in touch with the original concrete events that speak out of the soft underside of the mind, echoing with the strange togetherness of everything alive.

*Notes*
*Bibliography*
*Name Index*
*Subject Index*

# Notes

## Preface

1. James Wayne Dye, "Heraclitus and the Future of Process Philosophy," in *Tulane Studies in Philosophy 23: Studies in Process Philosophy*, ed. R. C. Wittemore (The Hague: Martinus Nijhoff, 1974), p. 24.

2. David Bohm, *Wholeness and the Implicate Order* (London: Routledge and Kegan Paul, 1981), p. xi.

3. T. I. Stcherbatsky, *The Central Conception of Buddhism and the Meaning of the Word 'Dharma'* (Calcutta: Susil Gupta, 1956; reprint, Delhi: Indological Book House, 1970), p. 41.

4. Alfred North Whitehead, *Adventures of Ideas* (New York: Macmillan, 1933), pp. 246–47; *Modes of Thought* (New York: Free Press, 1966), p. 151.

5. Kenneth K. Inada, "Problematics of the Buddhist Nature of Self," in *Buddhist and Western Philosophy*, ed. Nathan Katz (Atlantic Highlands, N.J.: Humanities Press, 1981), p. 285, n. 1.

6. Guy Richard Welbon, *The Buddhist Nirvana and Its Western Interpreters* (Chicago: Univ. of Chicago Press, 1968), p. 255.

7. Rune E. A. Johansson, *The Psychology of Nirvana* (London: George Allen and Unwin, 1969), pp. 62, 83.

8. Dye, "Heraclitus and the Future of Process Philosophy," p. 26.

## 1. Buddhist Philosophy on a New Human Frontier

1. Nolan Pliny Jacobson, *Buddhism: The Religion of Analysis* (London: George Allen and Unwin, 1966; reprint, Carbondale: Southern Illinois Univ. Press, Arcturus Books, 1970), chap. 2.

2. See Robert N. Bellah, "The Historical Background of Unbelief," in *The Culture of Unbelief,* ed. R. Caporale and A. Grumelli (Berkeley and Los Angeles: Univ. of California Press, 1971), pp. 43–44.

3. John Dewey, "Qualitative Thought," in *On Experience, Nature, and Freedom,* ed. Richard J. Bernstein (New York: Liberal Arts Press, 1960), p. 198. Dewey's title, "Qualitative Thought," testifies to the fundamental role qualities play in his philosophy and reminds one of the influence of Charles Peirce's category of "Firstness." In his essay on Peirce's "Firstness," Dewey comments that Peirce, "above all modern philosophers, has opened the road which permits a truly experiential philosophy to be developed which does not, like traditional empirical philosophies, cut experience off from nature" (Peirce's Theory of Quality," in *On Experience, Nature, and Freedom,* ed. Richard J. Bernstein [New York: Liberal Arts Press, 1960], pp. 209–10).

4. See Alfred North Whitehead, *The Function of Reason* (Boston: Beacon Press, 1958), p. 2, for his statement that the function of reason is to foster life.

5. K. Venkata Ramanan, *Nāgārjuna's Philosophy: As Presented in the Mahā-Prajñāparamitā-Sāstra* (Tokyo: Charles E. Tuttle for Harvard-Yenching Institute, 1962), pp. 38, 248.

6. Bhikkhu Ñānananda, *Concept and Reality in Early Buddhist Thought* (Kandy, Sri Lanka: Buddhist Publication Society, 1971), p. 75.

7. Victor Lowe, *Understanding Whitehead* (Baltimore: Johns Hopkins Univ. Press, 1962), p. 20.

8. John Dewey, *Art as Experience* (New York: G. P. Putnam's Sons, 1934), pp. 33, 34.

9. John Dewey, *Reconstruction in Philosophy* (Boston: Beacon Press, 1957), p. xii.

10. Henri Bergson, *Mind-Energy,* trans. H. Wildon Carr (New York: Henry Holt, 1920), pp. 31–32.

11. Quoted in Alexandra David-Neel and Lama Yongden, *The Secret Oral Teachings in Tibetan Buddhist Sects*, trans. H. N. M. Hardy (San Francisco: City Lights Books, 1967), p. 120.

12. Kitarō Nishida, "Affective Feeling," in *Japanese Phenomenology: Philosophy as a Transcultural Approach*, ed. Yoshihiro Nitta, Hirotaka Tatematsu, and Eiichi Shimomissē (Dordrecht, Holland: D. Reidel, 1979), pp. 67, 207–21.

13. Alfred North Whitehead, *Process and Reality*, ed. David Ray Griffin and Donald Sherburne (New York: Free Press, 1978), p. 7.

14. Kitarō Nishida, *Fundamental Problems of Philosophy*, trans. David Dilworth (Tokyo: Sophia Univ., 1970), pp. 45ff., 249, 252; also "The Problem of Japanese Culture," in *Sources of Japanese Tradition*, ed. R. Tsunoda, W. T. de Bary, and Donald Keene (New York: Columbia Univ. Press, 1958), pp. 867ff.

15. See Erich Fromm, *The Heart of Man* (New York: Harper and Row, 1964), pp. 58–59.

16. T. R. V. Murti, *The Central Philosophy of Buddhism*, 2d ed. (London: George Allen and Unwin, 1960), p. 58.

17. *Udana* 8, in *Minor Anthologies of the Pali Canon*, vol. 2, trans. F. L. Woodward (London: Oxford Univ. Press, 1948), p. 98.

18. The primary fact about Buddhism is its process-centered perspective, its unambiguous effort to help men and women overcome the suffering that stems from their inability to cope with the natural flow of the richness of life in the momentary nows that alone are the ground floor of the living world. Little children live this moment-to-moment, present-centered sense of being in direct touch with reality; "their concrete embodiment of a full life," as Kenneth K. Inada puts it, has not yet been displaced by the compulsions and proprietary concerns of an illusory self and a culture-encapsulated world. (Their natural feeling in the middle of the night, talking out of their sleep, is normally this: "I can't wait until tomorrow.") Because the child is not yet hampered by the artificial preoccupations of self-centered and substance-oriented cultural cocoons, "he or she perceives in a pure, clear, direct and total way, in touch with reality at all times; once distractions are removed, there is an instantaneous return to the former nature with its qualitative flow" (Kenneth K. Inada, "Nāgārjuna and

Beyond," *Journal of Buddhist Philosophy* 2(1984): 68, 70–71). A recent book about *Children of War* shows that this is the case even under the conditions of war (Roger Rosenblatt, *Children of War* [Garden City, N.Y.: Doubleday, Anchor Books, 1983]).

19. Charles Hartshorne, *Creativity in American Philosophy* (Albany: State Univ. of New York Press, 1984), pp. 4, 282.


## 2. Process Philosophies East and West

1. Max H. Fisch, ed., *Classic American Philosophers* (Englewood Cliffs, N.J.: Prentice-Hall, 1951).

2. Whitehead, *Modes of Thought*, p. 32.

3. Nishida, *Fundamental Problems of Philosophy*, pp. 249–51.

4. Alfred North Whitehead, *Science and the Modern World* (New York: Macmillan, 1925), p. 18; *Modes of Thought*, p. 62. Whitehead was writing perspectives such as these a quarter century before Heidegger came to the same point of view.

5. Whitehead, *Science and the Modern World*, pp. 55, 58.

6. Herbert V. Guenther, "Tasks Ahead," presidential address, Third Conference of the International Association of Buddhist Studies, Winnipeg, Canada, Aug. 1980, *Journal of the International Association of Buddhist Studies* 4 (1981): 118–19, 120.

7. Whitehead, *Adventures of Ideas*, p. 233; Charles Hartshorne, *Creative Synthesis and Philosophic Method* (LaSalle, Ill.: Open Court, 1970), p. 204; William James, *The Varieties of Religious Experience* (New York: Longmans, Green, 1902), p. 502; T. I. Stcherbatsky, *The Conception of Buddhist Nirvana* (Leningrad: Publishing Office of the Academy of Sciences, USSR, 1927), p. 54. As I have indicated in the Preface, Stcherbatsky had no explicit and systematic process philosophy available to him and thus could not see that what he was saying constituted reality at large, the social character of the world.

8. Stcherbatsky, *Central Conception of Buddhism*, p. 63.

9. Herbert V. Guenther, *Matrix of Mystery* (Boulder, Colo.: Shambhala, 1984), pp. 27, 5.

10. Kitarō Nishida, *Intelligibility and the Philosophy of Nothingness*, trans. Robert Schinzinger (Honolulu: East-West Center Press, 1966), pp. 158, 164, 171.

11. A. K. Warder, "Is Nāgārjuna a Mahāyānist?" in *The Problem of Two Truths in Buddhism and Vedānta*, ed. Mervyn Sprung (Dordrecht, Holland: D. Reidel, 1973), pp. 83, 85; Ramanan, *Nāgārjuna's Philosophy*, p. 276.

12. Toshihiko Izutsu, *Toward a Philosophy of Zen Buddhism* (Teheran: Imperial Iranian Academy of Philosophy, 1977), p. 106; David-Neel and Yongden, *Secret Oral Teachings*, pp. 50, 62.

13. G. P. Malalasekera, ed., *Encyclopedia of Buddhism* (Colombo, Sri Lanka: Government Press, 1961), 1:139.

14. Ibid.; Herbert V. Guenther, *Philosophy and Psychology in the Abhidharma* (Berkeley: Shambhala, 1974), p. 95. In my *Buddhism and the Contemporary World: Change and Self-Correction* (Carbondale: Southern Illinois Univ. Press, 1983), chap. 4, I call the concept of nirvana itself "the aesthetic center of life."

15. Ramanan, *Nāgārjuna's Philosophy*, pp. 38, 247–48.

16. David-Neel and Yongden, *Secret Oral Teachings*, pp. 120, 94.

17. *The Book of the Gradual Sayings (Aṅguttara-Nikāya)* 1: 172–73.

18. Clifford Geertz, "The Impact of the Concept of Culture," in *New Views of the Nature of Man*, ed. John R. Platt (Chicago: Univ. of Chicago Press, 1965), pp. 107–8.

19. Charles Hartshorne, *Insights and Oversights of Great Thinkers: An Evaluation of Western Philosophy* (Albany: State Univ. of New York Press, 1983), p. 28.

20. Christmas Humphreys, ed., vol. 3 of *Encyclopedia of Buddhism* (Colombo, Sri Lanka: Government Press, 1972), p. 348.

21. W. Howard Wriggins, *Ceylon: Dilemma of a New Nation* (Princeton: Princeton Univ. Press, 1960), p. 190.

22. Nestle quoted in Karl Popper, *The Open Society and Its Enemies*, 5th ed. (Princeton: Princeton Univ. Press, 1966), 1:12, 205.

23. Friedrich Nietzsche, *Philosophy and Truth: Selections from Nietzsche's Notebooks of the Early 1870s*, ed. and trans. Daniel Breazeale (Atlantic Highlands, N.J.: Humanities Press, 1979), p. 62.

24. Ibid., pp. 63, 64.

25. Heraclitus quoted in Dye, "Heraclitus and the Future of Process Philosophy," p. 27. According to Dye, Pythagoras was the

first to use the term "process philosophy." There are reasons for believing that in their contemporary American form most process philosophers, having been diverted by a preoccupation with cosmology and theology, have forgotten the historic insights of Heraclitus, who probed the fundamental modes of experience.

26. Kenneth Maly, "Man and Disclosure," in *Heraclitean Fragments: A Companion Volume to the Heidegger/Fink Seminar*, ed. Kenneth Maly and John Sallis (University, Ala.: Univ. of Alabama Press, 1980), pp. 56–57 (emphasis in original).

27. Dye, "Heraclitus and the Future of Process Philosophy," p. 26; Heraclitus quoted in Maly and Sallis, *Heraclitean Fragments*, p. 13 (Fragment 72).

28. Maly, "Man and Disclosure," in *Heraclitean Fragments*, ed. Maly and Sallis, pp. 55–57, 60. See Karl Popper, *The Open Society and Its Enemies* 1:15.

29. Dye, "Heraclitus and the Future of Process Philosophy," pp. 28, 26–27.

30. Popper, *The Open Society and Its Enemies* 1:12.

31. Popper, *The Open Society and its Enemies* 1:192; see also 1:18, 142.

32. Giovanni Reale, *The Systems of the Hellenistic Age*, ed. and trans. John R. Catan, vol. 3 of *A History of Ancient Philosophy*, 3 vols. (Albany: State Univ. of New York Press, 1985), pp. 88, 107.

33. Wladyslaw Tatarkiewicz, *History of Aesthetics*, ed. J. Harrell (Warsaw: PWN–Polish Scientific Publishers; The Hague: Mouton, 1970), 2:1.

34. Hartshorne, *Creativity in American Philosophy*, p. 253; *Creative Synthesis and Philosophic Method*, pp. 88, 177.

35. Charles Hartshorne, letter to author, June 10, 1978.

36. Hartshorne, *Insights and Oversights of Great Thinkers*, p. 365.

37. Hartshorne, *Creativity in American Philosophy*, p. 86.

38. Charles Hartshorne, "Introduction: The Development of Process Philosophy," in *Philosophers of Process*, ed. Douglas Browning (New York: Random House, 1965), pp. vii–xix.

39. Hartshorne, *Insights and Oversights of Great Thinkers*, p. 89.

40. Ibid., p. xvii.

41. John Dewey, *Experience and Nature,* 2d ed. (LaSalle, Ill.: Open Court, 1929), p. 138.

42. Charles Sanders Peirce, *Collected Papers of Charles Sanders Peirce,* vols. 1–6 ed. Charles Hartshorne and Paul Weiss, vols. 7 and 8 ed. A. W. Burke (Cambridge: Harvard Univ. Press, 1931–35, 1958), vol. 1, par. 357; vol. 5, par. 462; vols. 7, pars. 538–40.

43. Whitehead, *Modes of Thought,* p. 58.

44. William James, *The Writings of William James,* ed. John J. McDermott (New York: Random House, Modern Library, 1968), pp. 7–8 (diary entries of Feb. 1 and Apr. 30, 1870); Peirce, *Collected Papers,* vol. 1, par. 357; vol. 5, par. 382; Whitehead, *Process and Reality,* p. 339.

45. Donald Cary Williams, "Probability, Induction, and the Provident Man," in *Philosophic Thought in France and the United States,* ed. Marvin Farber (Albany: State Univ. of New York Press, 1968), p. 525.

46. Alfred North Whitehead, *Science and Philosophy* (Paterson, N.J.: Littlefield, Adams, 1964), pp. 225, 226, 228, 235.

47. Ludwig Wittgenstein, *Philosophical Investigations,* trans. G. E. M. Anscombe (Oxford: Basil Blackwell and Mott, 1958), p. 109.

48. Whitehead, *Science and Philosophy,* 235; Whitehead, *Adventures of Ideas,* p. 299; Hartshorne, *Creative Synthesis and Philosophic Method,* p. 300; Whitehead, *Science and Philosophy,* pp. 358–59.

49. Peirce, *Collected Papers,* vol. 2, par. 654.

50. Dewey, *Reconstruction in Philosophy.*

51. Whitehead, *Modes of Thought,* p. 151. See Charles Hartshorne, *Whitehead's Philosophy: Selected Essays, 1935–1970* (Lincoln: Univ. of Nebraska Press, 1972), p. 178. See also an undated Hartshorne response to my letter of March 26, 1975, on the concepts constituting the core of Whiteheadianism. Also Dye, "Heraclitus and the Future of Process Philosophy," p. 27: Dye comments on the preoccupation of so much contemporary Whiteheadian scholarship with his concept of God, arguing that this carries us far afield from the world of immediate experience where reality is found in "its creative advance."

52. Whitehead, *Process and Reality*, p. 21.

53. Charles Hartshorne, "Whitehead's Revolutionary Concept of Prehension," *International Philosophical Quarterly* 19 (Sep. 1979): 257.

54. Nolan Pliny Jacobson, "The Uses of Reason in Religion," *Iliff Review* 15 (Spring 1958): 57.

55. Hartshorne, *Insights and Oversights of Great Thinkers*, p. 344.

56. Guenther, *Matrix of Mystery*, p. 5.

57. Charles Hartshorne, *The Logic of Perfection* (LaSalle, Ill.: Open Court, 1962), p. 273.

58. Charles Hartshorne, "The Structure of Givenness," *Philosophical Forum* 18 (1960–61): 31.

59. Nolan Pliny Jacobson, "Whitehead and Buddhism on the Art of Living," *Eastern Buddhist* 8 (Oct. 1975): 7–36.

60. Kenneth K. Inada, "Whitehead's 'actual entities' and the Buddha's 'anatman'," *Philosophy East and West* 21 (July 1971): 303.

61. See Hartshorne, "The Structure of Givenness."

62. Hartshorne, *Insights and Oversights of Great Thinkers*, p. 42.

63. Victor Lowe, "The Concept of Experience in Whitehead's Metaphysics," in *Alfred North Whitehead: Essays in His Philosophy*, ed. George L. Kline (Englewood Cliffs, N.J.: Prentice-Hall, 1963), p. 132.

64. Alphonse de Waelhens, "Notes on Some Trends of Contemporary Philosophy," *Diogenes* 5 (Winter 1959): 39 (emphasis in original).

## 3. The Two Faces of Reason

1. Alfred North Whitehead, *Essays in Science and Philosophy* (New York: Philosophical Library, 1948), p. 121; R. G. Collingwood, *An Essay on Metaphysics* (New York: Oxford Univ. Press, 1940), pp. 47–48; Alan Sheridan, *Michel Foucault: The Will to Truth* (London: Tavistock, 1980), pp. 54, 196, 214.

2. Whitehead, *Process and Reality*, p. 166; Hartshorne, "Whitehead's Revolutionary Concept of Prehension," p. 258.

3. Because the term "process philosophy" is relatively new in the West, most philosophers do not think of themselves under this category. Peirce, for example, preferred to see himself working in the fields of logic, linguistics, philology, history, mathematics, and the natural sciences. It will take a long time for philosophers of many different self- and cultural images to see in process thinking what most of them would insist is the starting point of all critical interest in the nature of our experience in the world— namely, the observation that momentary occasions of experience are the really real things and contain within themselves the creativity that changes the world, all statements about the world being abstractions from this.

4. Hartshorne, "The Structure of Givenness," p. 22.

5. Hartshorne, *Creative Synthesis and Philosophic Method,* pp. 76–77; Whitehead, *Adventures of Ideas,* p. 225; Henri Bergson, *Creative Evolution,* trans. Arthur Mitchell (New York: Henry Holt, 1911), pp. 5, 165 (emphasis in original).

6. Victor Lowe, "The Concept of Experience in Whitehead's Metaphysics," p. 126.

7. Edmund Leach, *A Runaway World?* (New York: Oxford Univ. Press, 1968), p. 87.

8. Whitehead, *Modes of Thought,* p. 58; *Science and Philosophy,* p. 228.

9. Hegel's "concrete universal" reveals his confusion over the nature of concreteness.

10. Hartshorne, *Insights and Oversights of Great Thinkers,* pp. 25, 58. This is the basis in Greece for what Hartshorne calls "a general bias in philosophy and religion all over the world and through the centuries against the idea of undergoing influence, or of being in any way dependent upon others" ("Introduction: The Development of Process Philosophy," p. v).

11. Harry Austryn Wolfson, *Studies in the History of Philosophy and Religion,* ed. Isadore Twersky and George H. Williams (Cambridge: Harvard Univ. Press, 1973), pp. 107–8. Aristotle wanted an independent deity living without knowledge of earth's creatures since knowledge of them would have made God dependent upon the details of the world. Medieval theology changed this in order to declare that God knows all things, but no effort was made to refute Aristotle's religiously irrelevant deity. Harts-

horne calls this "cheating" and adds: "Aquinas had a God knowing all truth, but had no intelligible concept of knowledge to use theologically. Every moment of life we assume more or less consciously that the future is a matter of options, possibilities, limited by certain impossibilities and necessities. The sheer denial of contingency is contradicted pragmatically, whatever words we use. If we do not know what possibility (irreducible to necessity) is, we know nothing much metaphysically" (unpublished paper on Nāgārjuna delivered in Honolulu in August 1984, sent to me October 8).

12. Jacques Derrida, *Writing and Difference*, trans. Alan Bass (Chicago: Univ. of Chicago Press, 1978), pp. 81–82. Derrida was born into a Sephardic Jewish family living in El Biar, a suburb of Algiers.

13. Kevin Robb, "Preliterate Ages and the Linguistic Art of Heraclitus," in *Language and Thought in Early Greek Philosophy*, ed. Kevin Robb (LaSalle, Ill.: Hegeler Institute, 1983), p. 158.

14. Wallace Matson, "From Water to Atoms: The Triumph of Metaphysics," in *Language and Thought in Early Greek Philosophy*, ed. Kevin Robb (LaSalle, Ill.: Hegeler Institute, 1983), p. 255.

15. Reale, *The Systems of the Hellenistic Age*, p. 371.

16. Nestle quoted in Popper, *The Open Society and Its Enemies* 1:12, 205.

17. *Philoctetes*, 11. 448–52, in *Ten Greek Plays in Contemporary Translations*, ed. L. R. Lind, trans. Kathleen Freeman (Boston: Houghton Mifflin, 1957), p. 175.

18. William Wordsworth, *The Prelude*, 10:807–11.

19. George Wilhelm Friedrich Hegel, *Philosophy of History*, trans. J. Sibree (New York: Dover, 1956), p. 447. Another translation of the passage: "Never before since the sun has been in the sky and the planets have turned around it, had man stood on his head, i.e., based himself on the idea and constructed reality according to it. . . . It was a superb sunrise" (Jean Hyppolite, *Genesis and Structure of Hegel's* Phenomenology of Spirit, trans. Samuel Cherniak and John Heckman [Evanston, Ill.: Northwestern Univ. Press, 1974], p. 427).

20. Peirce, *Collected Papers*, vol. 5, par. 37; Hartshorne, *Whitehead's Philosophy*, p. 5.

21. See Bellah, "The Historical Background of Unbelief."

22. Wittgenstein, *Philosophical Investigations*, p. 101; see also pp. 103, 107.

23. Whitehead, *The Function of Reason*, p. 2.

24. Whitehead, *Science and the Modern World*, pp. 43, 2.

25. J. C. Crowther, *Founders of British Science* (London: Cresset Press, 1960), p. 268.

26. See, for example, E. W. Caspari and R. E. Marshak, "The Rise and Fall of Lysenko," *Science* 149(1965): 275–78.

27. David Lee Miller, *Philosophy of Creativity* (forthcoming), chap. 6.

28. Peirce, *Collected Papers*, vol. 1, par. 357; see also vol. 5, par. 462; vol. 6, pars. 143, 225, 229; vol. 7, par. 540.

29. George Schrader, "The Philosophy of Existence," in *The Philosophy of Kant and Our Modern World*, ed. Charles W. Hendel (New York: Liberal Arts Press, 1957), p. 37. See also Marjorie Grene, *The Knower and the Known* (New York: Basic Books, 1966), pp. 224ff.

30. Lewis P. Hinchman, *Hegel's Critique of the Enlightenment* (Gainesville: Univ. of Florida Press, 1984), p. 122.

31. Fichte and Schelling quoted in ibid., pp. 35, 37. In some ways Schelling's absolute resembles Plato's idea of the Good, which constitutes all specific goods but must be apprehended by the deepest cognitive thrust.

32. Martin Heidegger, *Hegel's Concept of Experience*, trans. K. R. Dove (New York: Octagon Books, 1983), p. 146.

33. Hartshorne, *Insights and Oversights of Great Thinkers*, p. 198.

34. Karl Marx, *Capital: A Critique of Political Economy*, trans. Samuel Moore and Edward Aveling (Chicago: Charles H. Kerr, 1906), 1:25.

35. George Santayana, "The Two Idealisms: A Dialogue in Limbo," in *The Process of Philosophy*, ed. Joseph Epstein and Gail Kennedy (New York: Random House, 1967), p. 510.

36. Karl Marx, "On the Jewish Question," in *The Marx-Engels Reader*, ed. Robert C. Tucker (New York: W. W. Norton, 1972), pp. 44–45.

37. Lucien Goldmann, *Lukacs and Heidegger: Toward a New Philosophy*, trans. William Q. Boelhower (London: Routledge and Kegan Paul, 1977), p. 30.

38. Søren Kierkegaard, *Concluding Unscientific Postscript,* trans. David Swenson (Princeton: Princeton Univ. Press, 1941), pp. 255, 266, 318.

39. See Nolan Pliny Jacobson, *Understanding Buddhism* (Carbondale: Southern Illinois Univ. Press, 1986), chap. 7.

40. Carnap quoted in J. O. Urmson, *Philosophical Analysis: Its Development Between the Two World Wars* (New York: Oxford Univ. Press, 1967), p. 124.

41. Richard Rorty, *Philosophy and the Mirror of Nature* (Princeton: Princeton Univ. Press, 1979), p. 380.

42. Whitehead, *Process and Reality,* p. 209.

43. Henri Bergson, *Creative Mind,* trans. M. L. Andison (New York: Philosophical Library, 1946), pp. 246–47.

44. Marvin Farber, "Descriptive Philosophy and Human Existence," in *Philosophic Thought in France and the United States,* ed. Marvin Farber (Albany: State Univ. of New York Press, 1968), p. 435.

45. J. Claude Piguet, *De l'Esthétique à la Métaphysique* (The Hague: Martinus Nijhoff, 1959), p. 215.

46. Albert Hofstadter, Introduction to *Poetry, Language, and Thought,* by Martin Heidegger, trans. Albert Hofstadter (New York: Harper and Row, 1971), pp. ix–x.

47. Hartshorne, *Insights and Oversights of Great Thinkers,* p. 239; Robert Magliola, *Derrida on the Mend* (West Lafayette, Ind.: Purdue Univ. Press, 1984), p. 57; Martin Heidegger, "Letter on Humanism," in *Basic Writings,* ed. and trans. David Farrell Krell (New York: Harper and Row, 1977), p. 206.

48. Martin Heidegger, *Nietzsche,* trans. David Farrell Krell (New York: Harper and Row, 1979), 1:5; Hartshorne, *Insights and Oversights of Great Thinkers,* p. 63.

49. Alfred North Whitehead, *The Philosophy of Alfred North Whitehead,* ed. P. A. Schilpp (New York: Tudor, 1941), p. 324.

50. Benjamin Lee Whorf, *Language, Thought, and Reality: Selected Writings of Benjamin Lee Whorf,* ed. J. B. Carroll (Cambridge: MIT Press, 1956), pp. 253–54.

51. Peirce quoted in Sandra B. Rosenthal, "Meaning as Habit: Some Systematic Implications of Peirce's Pragmatism," in *The Relevance of Charles Peirce,* ed. Eugene Freeman (LaSalle, Ill.: Hegeler Institute, 1983), p. 324.

52. Peirce lived most of his life in retirement. His obituary in the *Nation* states that in 1887 he retired to Pike County, Pa., where, until his death, April 23, 1914, "his only companion was his wife, who, before her marriage, was Juliette Froissy." This takes on added meaning in the light of the remark that follows, indicating that he felt "hunted like a wolf."

53. Peirce, *Collected Writings*, vol. 5, par. 386.

54. Hartshorne, *The Logic of Perfection*, p. 240.

55. Ramanan, *Nāgārjuna's Philosophy*, pp. 247–48; Whitehead, *The Function of Reason*, p. 2.


## 4. Nāgārjuna

1. Leroy Finch, "Introductory Remarks on Nāgārjuna Conference," *Journal of Buddhist Philosophy* 2 (1984): 50.

2. Alfonso Verdu, *The Philosophy of Buddhism* (The Hague: Martinus Nijhoff, 1981), pp. 106–7.

3. Ramanan, *Nāgārjuna's Philosophy*, p. 43.

4. Vicente Fatone, *The Philosophy of Nāgārjuna*, trans. D. Prithipaul (Delhi: Motilal Banarsidass, 1981), p. 25.

5. Whitehead, *Process and Reality*, p. 166.

6. K. Satchidananda Murty, *Nāgārjuna* (New Delhi: National Book Trust, 1971), pp. 57, 67.

7. P. V. Bapat, ed., *Twenty-Five Hundred Years of Buddhism*, rev. ed. (New Delhi: Government of India, 1976), pp. 194–95; Thomas Berry, *Buddhism* (New York: Hawthorne Books, 1967), p. 150 (Berry argues that Nāgārjuna's *Mūlamadhyamakakārikā* "is the most powerful thought system evolved in the entire history of Buddhism"); Karl Jaspers, *The Great Philosophers*, ed. Hannah Arendt, trans. Ralph Manheim (New York: Harcourt, Brace and World, 1957); T. R. V. Murti, *The Central Philosophy of Buddhism*, p. 4; Daisaku Ikeda, *Buddhism: The First Millennium*, trans. Burton Watson (Tokyo: Kodansha International, 1977), p. 138.

8. M. Walleser, *The Life of Nāgārjuna from Tibetan and Chinese Sources* (Delhi: Asia Major, 1923).

9. Ikeda, *Buddhism*, p. 98.

10. Herbert V. Guenther, letter to author, Feb. 22, 1986; Chr.

Lindtner, *Nagarjuniana* (Copenhagen: Akademisk Forlag, 1982), pp. 9–18.

11. Alex Wayman, "Who Understands the Four Alternatives of the Buddhist Texts?" *Philosophy East and West* 27 (Jan. 1977): 3–21.

12. Jaspers, *The Great Philosophers*, p. 7.

13. Ibid., p. 424.

14. Chandradhar Sharma, *Dialectic in Buddhism and Vedānta* (Banaras, India: Nand Kishore and Bros., 1952), pp. 12, 16, 266.

15. S. Radhakrishnan, *Indian Philosophy* (London: George Allen and Unwin, 1923), 1:697, 699, 697–703.

16. Efforts to absorb Buddhism in the Upaniṣadic fold show no signs of abating. Raymond Panikkar repeats the refusal of Indian thought to reconceive itself in process terms. "Either what 'is' is and then cannot become, come to be, because it already is; or what 'is' is not, because we can nowhere find such an 'is.' It is pure transcendence. And this is the *ātman* as well as the *anātman*. It does not matter at all if pure unrelatedness is or is-not. Change is not possible because Being is immutable." These are Panikkar's words in dealing with what he conceives to be "the crisis" in Budhist and Indian philosophy today (Raymond Panikkar, "The 'crisis' of Mādhyamika and Indian Philosophy Today," *Philosophy East and West* 16 [1966]: 129). From a Buddhist point of view, the "crisis" originates in the attempt to view the universe from a standpoint beyond it, treating it in this way as something less than a universe.

17. Hajime Nakamura, *Indian Buddhism* (Osaka: Kansai Univ. of Foreign Studies, 1980), pp. 244, 212.

18. Saṅkara quoted in Sharma, *Dialectic in Buddhism and Vedānta*, p. 169.

19. Ibid., p. 14.

20. Ramanan, *Nāgārjuna's Philosophy*, p. 171.

21. Ibid., pp. 338–39, 342, 138.

22. Ibid., p. 173.

23. Hartshorne, *Creative Synthesis and Philosophic Method*, p. xvii.

24. Hartshorne, "Whitehead's Revolutionary Concept of Prehension," p. 257; Ramanan, *Nāgārjuna's Philosophy*, p. 38; Guenther, *Matrix of Mystery*, p. 40.

25. Junjirō Takakusu, *The Essentials of Buddhist Philosophy*, ed. Wing-tsit Chan and Charles A. Moore (Westport, Conn.: Greenwood Press, 1975), p. 197; Hemanta Kumar Ganguli, *Philosophy of Logical Construction* (Calcutta: Sanskrit Pustak Bhandar, 1963), p. 208; Vidushekhara Bhattacharya, *The Basic Conception of Buddhism* (Calcutta: Univ. of Calcutta, 1934), p. 83; R. Puligandla, *Fundamentals of Indian Philosophy* (Lanham, Md.: Univ. Press of America, 1985), p. 88; Hartshorne, *Insights and Oversights of Great Thinkers*, p. 198.

26. Whitehead, *Process and Reality*, p. 4.

27. Nakamura, *Indian Buddhism*, p. 248.

28. Ramanan, *Nāgārjuna's Philosophy*, p. 264.

29. *Majjhima-Nikāya* quoted in Kamaleswar Bhattacharya, *The Dialectical Method of Nagarjuna (Vigrahavyāvartanī)* (Delhi: Motilal Banarsidass, 1978), pp. 36–37.

30. Welbon, *Buddhist Nirvana*, p. 304; Karl Potter, *Presuppositions of India's Philosophies* (Westport, Conn.: Greenwood Press, 1977), p. 238; Whitehead, *Science and the Modern World*, p. 18.

31. Warder, "Is Nāgārjuna a Mahāyānist?" p. 85 (Warder is referring here to the *Mūlamadhyamakakārika*).

32. David-Neel and Yongden, *Secret Oral Teachings*, p. 72.

33. Takakusu, *The Essentials of Buddhist Philosophy*, p. 123; Whitehead, *Process and Reality*, p. 21.

34. David-Neel and Yongden, *Secret Oral Teachings*, pp. 50–51.

35. Warder, "Is Nāgārjuna a Mahāyānist? p. 85. Warder is defending the views of the *Tripiṭaka*, "an empiricist type of philosophy consisting of the four noble truths and conditioned origination, presented as empirical discoveries which the Buddha has made and anyone can verify for himself" (p. 85).

36. Peirce, *Collected Papers*, vol. 1, par. 357. See also vol. 5, par. 462, and vol. 7, pars. 538–40.

37. Ibid., vol. 5, par. 462; vol. 7, pars. 538–40.

38. Hartshorne, *Creativity in American Philosophy*, p. 106.

39. David-Neel and Yongden, *Secret Oral Teachings*, p. 34.

40. Milton Singer, *Man's Glassy Essence: Explorations in Semiotic Anthropology* (Bloomington: Indiana Univ. Press, 1984), pp. 3, 494, 501.

41. Gilbert Ryle, *The Concept of the Mind* (New York: Barnes and Noble, 1949).

42. Peirce, *Collected Papers*, vol. 6, par. 134; vol. 5, pars. 549–604. I have quoted here from Peirce's famous letter to Lady Welby of December 23, 1908. See also Charles S. Hardwick, ed., *Semiotic and Significs: The Correspondence Between Charles S. Peirce and Victoria Lady Welby* (Bloomington: Indiana Univ. Press, 1977), p. 73.

43. Peirce, *Collected Papers*, vol. 5, pars. 549–604.

44. Whitehead, *Process and Reality*, p. 310.

45. Whitehead, *Adventures of Ideas*, p. 220.

46. Bellah, "The Historical Background of Unbelief," pp. 43–44.

47. Whitehead, *Adventures of Ideas*, p. 220.

48. Heidegger, *Hegel's Concept of Experience*, pp. 119–20, 112, 130, 134.

49. Friedrich Nietzsche, *The Birth of Tragedy*, trans. F. Golffing (Garden City, N.Y.: Doubleday, 1956), p. 93.

50. F. S. C. Northrop, *Man, Nature, and God* (New York: Simon and Schuster, 1962), p. 19. Whitehead had left Cambridge and was located at the Imperial College of Science and Technology in South Kensington.

51. Ibid., pp. 185–86.

52. Hartshorne, *Insights and Oversights of Great Thinkers*, pp. 355, 348.

53. Bohm, *Wholeness and the Implicate Order.*

54. Kenneth K. Inada, *Nāgārjuna: A Translation of His Mūlamadhyamakakārika with an Introductory Essay* (Tokyo: Hokuseido Press, 1970), pp. 39, 17; Lama Anagarika Govinda, *Creative Meditation and Multi-Dimensional Consciousness* (Wheaton, Ill.: Theosophical Publishing House, 1976), p. 105.

55. T. R. V. Murti uses Immanuel Kant to find in Buddhism and explicate for Western readers this kind of transcendent realm *(The Central Philosophy of Buddhism)*. Edward Conze does the same; see his *Buddhism: Its Essence and Development* (Oxford: Bruno Cassirer, 1951), and *Buddhist Thought in India* (London: George Allen and Unwin, 1961).

56. Inada, *Nāgārjuna*, pp. 17–18.

57. Nāgārjuna quoted in Ikeda, *Buddhism*, p. 143.

58. Nāgārjuna quoted in Murti, *The Central Philosophy of Buddhism*, p. 164. See also Ramanan, *Nāgārjuna's Philosophy*, p. 96.

59. Lindtner, *Nagarjuniana,* p. 137; Alicia Matsunaga, *The Buddhist Philosophy of Assimilation* (Tokyo: Charles E. Tuttle and Sophia University, 1969), p. 71; Inada, "Problematics of the Buddhist Nature of Self," p. 276. See also p. 284: "It is an ontology that should not be confused with ontologies of the usual type, because it opens up the world as a continuum which is the basis for the compassionate and enlightened natures in man."

60. Welbon, *Buddhist Nirvana,* 304.

61. Page 22 of unpublished paper on Nāgārjuna delivered by Charles Hartshorne in Honolulu in August 1984, sent to me on October 8.

62. Mervyn Sprung, ed., *The Question of Being* (University Park, Pa.: Penn State Univ. Press, 1978), p. 11.

63. Kenneth K. Inada, "The Metaphysics of Cumulative Penetration Revisited," *Process Studies* 13 (Summer 1983): 156–57; Charles Hartshorne, Review of *Plato's Philosophy of History,* by Daniel A. Dombrowski, *Process Studies* 12 (Fall 1982): 202.

64. Hartshorne, "Whitehead's Revolutionary Concept of Prehension," pp. 254, 262.

65. Hartshorne, *Creativity in American Philosophy,* p. 80; Stcherbatsky, *The Conception of Buddhist Nirvana,* pp. 52, 54.

66. Recent research on the human brain indicates that this is the way it grows, through the evocation of deeper vividness and intensity of experience, multiplying the synapses in the cerebral cortex. Memory grows with more to remember, more to perceive, generating novel connections as the brain "branches out" (Stephen S. Hall, "Brain Branches Out," *Science 85* 6 [June 1985]: 72–74). The way of the bodhisattva appears in this new light to be solidly based on empirical fact, widening the range of his or her participation in a caring and suffering world, leading the Way by caring more inclusively for the ontological togetherness of life. Living this social nature of reality, the bodhisattva represents a higher state of conscious awareness than the species appears thus far to understand. Opening individuals to feel the world in its wider ranges of diversity, and in unparochial and unconventional ways, may well be the central key to human development.

67. Murti, *The Central Philosophy of Buddhism,* pp. 9, 11, 13, 14; Ninian Smart, *Doctrine and Argument in Indian Philosophy* (London: George Allen and Unwin, 1964), p. 213.

68. Conze, *Buddhist Thought in India*, pp. 24, 233.

69. Kamaleswar Bhattacharya, *The Dialectical Method of Nagarjuna*, pp. 1, 83; Ludwig Wittgenstein, *Tractatus Logico-Philosophicus* (London: Routledge and Kegan Paul, 1949), par. 6.44. See the personal reflections of F. S. C. Northrop in *Man, Nature, and God*, p. 243: During a sabbatical at Cambridge in 1932–33, Northrop thought he saw what Wittgenstein was saying "between the lines." In his essay entitled "Language, Mysticism, and God," Northrop concludes that "no words mean or say anything, except as one knows with inexpressible and unsayable immediacy, what the words are pointing at or showing, independently of the words themselves. Such knowledge is what the word 'mystical' means" (p. 241). "This is why the professed clarity of the present English ordinary language professors and lawyers is spurious" (p. 243). What Wittgenstein means by the mystical is the immediate experience of unsayable qualities illuminating the face of the world. There are remarks scattered through his writing suggesting deep frustration over his inability to break out of his linguistic cage. Northrop finds this his most remarkable contribution to modern thought: "In an age when laymen, scientists, and even most theologians had dismissed mysticism, as something, at best, having no meaning for them and, at worst, merely esoteric, purple prose nonsense, it was Wittgenstein's genius to have rediscovered that there is no knowledge of any kind that is not, in its elements, mystical" (p. 239).

## 5. Buddhism and Western Theology

1. Whitehead, *Process and Reality*, pp. 31, 222, 232.

2. Langdon Gilkey, "The Mystery of Being and Nonbeing: An Experimental Project," *Journal of Religion* 58 (Jan. 1978): 1, 12. These two quotations are the opening and closing lines of the John Nuveen Lecture in the Divinity School at the University of Chicago.

3. Ibid., p. 1.

4. Whitehead, *Modes of Thought*, p. 82.

5. Ludwig Wittgenstein, *Philosophische Bemerkungen*, ed. Rush Rhees (Oxford: Basil Blackwell and Mott, 1965). It is signifi-

cant that one of Wittgenstein's favorite philosophers was Kierke-gaard, who would have agreed that, as Wittgenstein puts it, "if Christianity is the truth then all the philosophy that has been written about it is false" (Ludwig Wittgenstein, *Culture and Value*, ed. G. H. Von Wright, trans. Peter Winch [Chicago: Univ. of Chicago Press, 1980], p. 83e).

6. John M. Koller, *Oriental Philosophies* (New York: Charles Scribner's Sons, 1970), pp. 192–93.

7. Guenther, *Philosophy and Psychology in the Abhidharma*, p. 95; Kenneth K. Inada, letter to author, Aug. 26, 1977; Kenneth K. Inada, "The Ultimate Ground of Buddhist Purification," in *Proceedings of the Eleventh International Congress of the International Association for the History of Religions* (Leiden, Holland: E. J. Brill, 1968), 1:146.

8. Alfred North Whitehead, *Religion in the Making* (Cleveland: World, 1926), p. 105. Josiah Royce and George Santayana are not in agreement with this statement.

9. Charles Hartshorne, "Toward a Buddhisto-Christian Religion," in *Buddhism and American Thinkers*, eds. Kenneth K. Inada and Nolan Pliny Jacobson (Albany: State Univ. of New York Press, 1984), pp. 12–13.

10. Dewey, *Art as Experience*, p. 195.

11. Dietrich Bonhoeffer, *Prisoner of God: Letters and Papers from Prison*, ed. Eberhard Bethge, trans. R. H. Fuller (New York: Macmillan, 1958), p. 167; Thomas J. J. Altizer, ed., *Towards a New Christianity: Readings in the Death of God Theology* (New York: Harcourt, Brace and World, 1967); Whitehead, *Process and Reality*, pp. 337–38; *Science and Philosophy*, p. 101; *Process and Reality*, p. 339.

12. J. Hillis Miller, *The Disappearance of God: Five Nineteenth-Century Writers* (Cambridge: Harvard Univ. Press, 1976).

13. Whitehead, *Science and the Modern World*, p. 18.

14. This new orientation to a "universe becoming increasingly alive" (Erich Jantsch, *The Self-Organizing Universe: Scientific and Human Implications of the Emerging Paradigm of Evolution* [Oxford: Pergamon Press, 1980], p. 189) is an organic part of the scientific breakthroughs of the silicon chip that have forced the ecclesiastical establishments of the West to join the community of humankind.

15. Inada, "The Metaphysics of Cumulative Penetration Revisited," pp. 156–57.

16. Hartshorne, *Creative Synthesis and Philosophic Method*, p. 204.

17. Malalasekera, ed., *Encyclopedia of Buddhism* 2:600.

18. Hartshorne, *Insights and Oversights of Great Thinkers*, p. 366.

19. Henry Nelson Wieman, *Man's Ultimate Commitment* (Carbondale: Southern Illinois Univ. Press, 1958); also *The Empirical Theology of Henry Nelson Wieman*, ed. Robert W. Bretall (New York: Macmillan, 1963; reprint, Carbondale: Southern Illinois Univ. Press, 1969).

20. Henry Nelson Wieman, "Science and a New Religious Reformation," *Zygon* 1 (June 1966): 125–39.

21. See Charles Sanders Peirce, *Charles Sanders Peirce: Contributions to the* Nation: *Part Two, 1894–1900*, compiled by Kenneth Laine Ketner and James Edward Cook, *Graduate Studies 16* (Lubbock: Texas Tech University, 1978).

22. Henry Nelson Wieman, "Intellectual Autobiography," Southern Illinois Univ. Archives, Carbondale, Ill., p. 22; also Wieman's *The Directive in History* (Glencoe, Ill.: Free Press, 1949), p. 30.

23. Henry Nelson Wieman, *The Source of Human Good* (Chicago: Univ. of Chicago Press, 1946; reprint, Southern Illinois Univ. Press, 1964), pp. 135, 136, 303–5.

24. Ibid., pp. 304–5.

25. Wieman, "Intellectual Autobiography," p. 28.

26. Robert Bretall, in Wieman, *Empirical Theology*, p. 210.

27. Henry Nelson Wieman, *The Wrestle of Religion with Truth* (New York: Macmillan, 1927), p. 191.

28. Henry Nelson Wieman and Regina Westcott-Wieman, *Normative Psychology of Religion* (New York: Thomas Y. Crowell, 1935), p. 180; also Wieman, *Man's Ultimate Commitment*, pp. 88–89.

29. Wieman, *Man's Ultimate Commitment*, p. 72.

30. Wieman, *Man's Ultimate Commitment*, chap. 3; David Lee Miller, letter to author, Sep. 2, 1984; David Lee Miller, "Buddhist Themes in Wieman's View of Creative Interchange," in

*Creative Interchange*, ed. John A. Broyer and William S. Minor (Carbondale: Southern Illinois Univ. Press, 1982), p. 419.

31. The Hara-Wieman correspondence is now in the Archives at Southern Illinois University at Carbondale, where Wieman taught in the Department of Philosophy the last ten years of his teaching career.

32. Wieman, "Intellectual Autobiography," pp. 2–3.

33. Ibid., p. 6.

34. Peirce, *Collected Papers*, vol. 5, par. 575.

35. Richard Fox, *Reinhold Niebuhr* (New York: Pantheon Books, 1986).

36. Reinhold Niebuhr, *The Nature and Destiny of Man* (New York: Charles Scribner's Sons, 1943), 2:299, 206, 307.

37. Ibid., pp. 110, 98.

38. Whitehead, *Science and the Modern World*, pp. 92–93.

39. Niebuhr, *Nature and Destiny of Man*, 2:74.

40. Ibid., pp. 72, 45.

41. Ibid., p. 8.

42. Ibid., p. 49.

43. Wieman, *Empirical Theology*, pp. 106–7.

44. Wieman, *Source of Human Good*, p. 309.

45. Wieman, *Empirical Theology*, pp. 132, 139.

46. Ibid.

47. Ibid., pp. 8–9.

48. William Sherman Minor, *Creativity in Henry Nelson Wieman* (Metuchen, N.J.: Scarecrow Press, 1977), pp. 165–92. See also S. Morris Eames, "Meaning, Value, and Creativity in Dewey and Wieman," in *Creative Interchange*, ed. John A. Broyer and William S. Minor (Carbondale: Southern Illinois Univ. Press, 1982), pp. 208–31.

49. John Dewey, *A Common Faith* (New Haven: Yale Univ. Press, 1934), p. 24.

50. Ibid., p. 87.

51. Ibid., pp. 52, 46.

52. J. N. Findlay, *The Transcendence of the Cave* (London: George Allen and Unwin, 1967), pp. 104–5.

53. Dye, "Heraclitus and the Future of Process Philosophy," p. 26.

54. Lowe, "The Concept of Experience in Whitehead's Metaphysics," p. 132.

55. Whitehead, *Modes of Thought,* pp. 151, 121.

56. Hartshorne, *Creative Synthesis and Philosophic Method,* pp. 87–88; Lowe, *Understanding Whitehead,* p. 328.

57. Hartshorne, "Whitehead's Revolutionary Concept of Prehension," p. 254; see also Charles Hartshorne, John Cobb, Jr., and Lewis S. Ford, "Three Responses to Neville's *Creativity and God," Process Studies* 10 (Fall–Winter 1980): 96.

58. Tape available at Southern Illinois Univ. Archives, Carbondale, Ill.

59. Inada, "The Metaphysics of Buddhist Experience and the Whiteheadian Encounter," *Philosophy East and West* 25 (Oct. 1975): 483; Whitehead, *Essays in Science and Philosophy,* p. 72; also Whitehead, *Science and Philosophy,* pp. 102, 125–26.

60. Hartshorne, *The Logic of Perfection,* pp. 131–32.

61. Hartshorne, "Toward a Buddhisto-Christian Religion," p. 5; *Creative Synthesis and Philosophic Method,* pp. xix–xx, xx–xxi.

62. Charles Hartshorne, "Whitehead's Differences from Buddhism," *Philosophy East and West* 25 (Oct. 1975): 408.

63. Hartshorne, "Toward a Buddhisto-Christian Religion," pp. 12–13.

64. Jacobson, *Understanding Buddhism;* Charles Hartshorne letter to Southern Illinois Univ. Press, Oct. 8, 1984.

65. Charles Hartshorne, letter to author, Oct. 8, 1984.

66. Charles Hartshorne, "Emptiness and Fullness in Asiatic and Western Thought," *Journal of Chinese Philosophy* 6 (1979): 419.

67. Grene, *The Knower and the Known,* p. 224.

## 6. *The Religion of Analysis and the Spirit of Modern Science*

1. Gunnar Myrdal, *Asian Drama: An Inquiry into the Poverty of Nations* (New York: Twentieth Century Fund, 1968), 1:702–3; Alfred North Whitehead, *The Aims of Education and Other Essays* (New York: Macmillan, 1929), pp. 22–23.

2. Karl Popper, *The Logic of Scientific Discovery* (New York: Harper and Row, 1959; Torchbook, 1965), p. 431.

3. Peirce, *Collected Papers*, vol. 2, par. 166.

4. Roger Sperry, *Values: Number One Problem of Our Times* (New York: Columbia Univ. Press, 1983), p. 10.

5. Ilya Prigogine, *From Being to Becoming* (San Francisco: W. H. Freeman, 1979), pp. 2–3.

6. Milič Čapek, "The Second Scientific Revolution," *Diogenes* 63 (1968): 125.

7. Joseph Needham, *Science and Civilization in China* (Cambridge: Cambridge Univ. Press, 1954).

8. Werner Heisenberg, *Physics and Philosophy: The Revolution in Modern Science* (New York: Harper and Bros., 1958), p. 202.

9. Atuhiro Sibatani, "The Japanese Brain," *Science 80* 1 (Dec. 1980): 22–27.

10. Seizo Ohe, "Scientific Creativity in Eastern Cultural Setting," *Annals of the Japanese Association for Philosophy of Science* 5 (Mar. 1979): 54.

11. Ibid., pp. 52, 53.

12. Kiyosi Yabuuti, "The Pre-History of Modern Science in Japan: The Importation of Western Science During the Tokugawa Period," *Cahiers d'Histoire Mondiale* 9 (1965): 218.

13. Hu Shih, "The Scientific Spirit and Method in Chinese Philosophy," in *The Chinese Mind*, ed. Charles A. Moore (Honolulu: East-West Center Press, 1967), p. 109.

14. Oggü quoted in Hajime Nakamura, "The Individual and the Universal," *The Japanese Mind: Essentials of Japanese Philosophy and Culture* (Honolulu: East-West Center Press, 1967), p. 188.

15. Peirce, *Collected Papers*, vol. 5, par. 373.

16. Robert Guillain, *The Japanese Challenge*, trans. Patrick O'Brian (New York: J. B. Lippincott, 1970), p. 25.

17. Ezra F. Vogel, *Japan as Number One* (Cambridge: Harvard Univ. Press, 1979), pp. 30, 18.

18. William K. Cummings, *Education and Equality in Japan* (Princeton: Princeton Univ. Press, 1980), p. 10.

19. Seizo Ohe, "Japan in a World-Historical Perspective," *Revue Internationale de Philosophie* 28 (1974): 35.

20. Chamnong Tongprasert, Royal Institute, Bangkok, Thailand, letter to author, Sep. 1, 1969.

21. Jeffrey Meyer, "Could Buddhist Insights Shape a Better World?" *Charlotte Observer*, Mar. 18, 1984.

22. Jacobson, *Buddhism and the Contemporary World*, p. 122.

## 7. The Civilization of Experience

1. Edward T. Hall, *Beyond Culture* (Garden City, N.Y.: Doubleday, Anchor Books, 1977), p. 240.

2. Robin Fox, *Encounter with Anthropology* (New York: Dell, 1968), p. 295.

3. Daniel Breazeale, *Introduction to Philosophy and Truth: Selections from Nietzsche's Notebooks of the Early 1870s* (Atlantic Highlands, N.J.: Humanities Press, 1979), p. xxvii.

4. Nietzsche quoted in ibid., p. xviii.

5. Arnold J. Toynbee, *Civilization on Trial* (New York: Oxford Univ. Press, 1948), pp. 222–23.

6. M. Rostovtzeff, *The Social and Economic History of the Roman Empire* (New York: Oxford Univ. Press, 1926), p. 487.

7. Nietzsche, *Philosophy and Truth*, p. 104.

8. Whitehead, *Science and Philosophy*, p. 73.

9. Kenneth K. Inada, "The American Involvement with Śūnyatā: Prospects," *Buddhism and American Thinkers*, ed. Kenneth K. Inada and Nolan Pliny Jacobson (Albany: State Univ. of New York Press, 1984), pp. 87–88.

10. See Donald Johanson and Maitland Edey, *Lucy: The Beginnings of Mankind* (New York: Simon and Schuster, Warner Books, 1981).

11. Richard E. Leakey and Roger Lewin, *People of the Lake: Mankind and Its Beginnings* (Garden City, N.Y.: Doubleday, Anchor Books, 1978), p. 256.

12. Fred Hoyle, *Highlights in Astronomy* (San Francisco: W. H. Freeman, 1975), pp. 131ff.

13. Edward T. Hall, *Beyond Culture*, p. 240.

14. Whitehead, *Science and Philosophy*, p. 235.

# Bibliography

## English Translations of Buddhist Texts

The largest volume and variety of Buddhist perspectives available
in English can be found in the publications of the Pali Text Society
in London. Comparatively few of the Sanskrit texts, according to
Herbert Guenther, survived the waves of destruction that swept
over the Indian subcontinent in the past two thousand years.

*The Book of the Discipline (Vinaya Piṭaka)*, Parts 1, 2, and 3 *(Sut-
tavibhaṅga)*. Translated by I. B. Horner. London: Oxford Univ.
Press, 1949, 1957.

*The Book of the Discipline*. Part 4 *(Mahāvagga)*. Translated by
I. B. Horner. London: Luzac, 1952.

*The Book of the Gradual Sayings (Aṅguttara-Nikāya)*. Vols. 1, 2,
and 5 translated by F. L. Woodward; vols. 3 and 4 translated by
E. M. Hare. London: Luzac, 1952, 1955.

*The Book of the Kindred Sayings (Saṃyutta-Nikāya)*. Vols. 1 and
2 translated by C. A. F. Rhys Davids; vols. 3, 4, and 5 translated
by F. L. Woodward. London: Luzac, 1950, 1953, 1954, 1956.

*Dialogues of the Buddha (Dīgha-Nikāya)*. Part 1. Translated by
T. W. Rhys Davids. London: Oxford Univ. Press, 1910. Reprint.
London: Luzac, 1959.

*Dialogues of the Buddha*. Part 2. Translated by T. W. and C. A. F.
Rhys Davids. London: Oxford Univ. Press, 1910. Reprint. London: Luzac, 1959.

*Dialogues of the Buddha*. Part 3. Translated by T. W. and C. A. F.
Rhys Davids. London: Luzac, 1957.

*Compendium of Philosophy (Abhidammattha-Sangaha)*. Translated by Shwe Zan Aung. London: Luzac, 1956.

*The Middle Length Sayings (Majjhima-Nikāya)*. 3 Vols. Translated by I. B. Horner. London: Luzac, 1954, 1957, 1959.

*The Minor Anthologies of the Pali Canon (Khuddaka-Nikāya)*. Vol. 1 *(Khuddaka-pātha: The Reading of Small Passages* and *Dhammapada: Words of the Doctrine)*. Translated by C. A. F. Rhys Davids. London: Oxford Univ. Press, 1931.

*The Minor Anthologies of the Pali Canon*. Vol. 2 *(Udāna: Verses of Uplift* and *Itivuttaka: As It Was Said)*. Translated by F. L. Woodward. London: Oxford Univ. Press, 1948.

*The Minor Anthologies of the Pali Canon*. Vol. 3 *(Buddhavamsa: The Lineage of the Buddhas* and *Cariyāpitaka: Collection of Ways of Conduct)*. Translated by B. C. Law. London: Oxford Univ. Press, 1938.

*The Minor Anthologies of the Pali Canon*. Vol. 4 *(Vimanavatthu: Stories of the Mansions* and *Petavatthu: Stories of the Departed)*. Translated by Jean Kennedy and H. S. Gehman, respectively. London: Luzac, 1942.

*The Questions of King Milinda*. Part 1. Translated by T. W. Rhys Davids. Sacred Books of the East, vols. 35–36. Oxford: Clarendon Press, 1890–1894. Reprint. New York: Dover, 1963.

*Woven Cadences of Early Buddhists (Suttanipāta)*. Translated by E. M. Hare. London: Oxford Univ. Press, 1947.

## Works Cited in Text

Altizer, Thomas J. J., ed. *Toward a New Christianity: Readings in the Death of God Theology*. New York: Harcourt, Brace and World, 1967.

Bapat, P. V., ed. *Twenty-Five Hundred Years of Buddhism*. Rev. ed. New Delhi: Government of India, 1976.

Bellah, Robert N. "The Historical Background of Unbelief." In *The Culture of Unbelief*, edited by R. Caporale and A. Grumelli, pp. 39–52. Berkeley and Los Angeles: Univ. of California Press, 1971.

Bergson, Henri. *Creative Evolution*. Translated by A. Mitchell. New York: Henry Holt, 1911.

_____. *Creative Mind*. Translated by M. L. Andison. New York: Philosophical Library, 1946.

_____. *Mind-Energy*. Translated by H. Wildon Carr. New York: Henry Holt, 1920.

Berry, Thomas. *Buddhism*. Twentieth-Century Encyclopedia of Catholicism, vol. 145. New York: Hawthorne Books, 1967.

Bhattacharya, Kamaleswar. *The Dialectical Method of Nagarjuna (Vigrahavyāvartani)*. Delhi: Motilal Banarsidass, 1978.

Bhattacharya, Vidushekhara. *The Basic Conception of Buddhism*. Calcutta: Univ. of Calcutta, 1934.

Bohm, David. *Wholeness and the Implicate Order*. London: Routledge and Kegan Paul, 1981.

Bonhoeffer, Dietrich. *Prisoner of God: Letters and Papers from Prison*. Edited by Eberhard Bethge. Translated by R. H. Fuller. New York: Macmillan, 1958.

Breazeale, Daniel. Introduction to *Philosophy and Truth: Selections from Nietzsche's Notebooks of the Early 1870s*. Edited and translated by Daniel Breazeale. Atlantic Highlands, N.J.: Humanities Press, 1979.

Čapek, Milič. "The Second Scientific Revolution." *Diogenes* 63 (1968): 114–33.

Caspari, E. W., and R. E. Marshak. "The Rise and Fall of Lysenko." *Science* 149 (1965): 275–78.

Collingwood, R. G. *An Essay on Metaphysics*. New York: Oxford Univ. Press, 1940.

Conze, Edward. *Buddhism: Its Essence and Development*. Oxford: Bruno Cassirer, 1951.

_____. *Buddhist Thought in India*. London: George Allen and Unwin, 1962.

Crowther, J. C. *Founders of British Science*. London: Cresset Press, 1960.

Cummings, William K. *Education and Equality in Japan*. Princeton: Princeton Univ. Press, 1980.

David-Neel, Alexandra, and Lama Yongden. *The Secret Oral Teachings in Tibetan Buddhist Sects*. Translated by H. N. M. Hardy. San Francisco: City Lights Books, 1967.

Derrida, Jacques. *Writing and Difference.* Translated by Alan Bass. Chicago: Univ. of Chicago Press, 1978.

Dewey, John. *Art as Experience.* New York: G. P. Putnam's Sons, 1934.

_____. *A Common Faith.* New Haven: Yale Univ. Press, 1934.

_____. *Experience and Nature.* 2d ed. LaSalle, Ill.: Open Court, 1929.

_____. "Peirce's Theory of Quality." In *On Experience, Nature, and Freedom,* edited by Richard J. Bernstein, pp. 199–210. New York: Liberal Arts Press, 1960.

_____. "Qualitative Thought." In *On Experience, Nature, and Freedom,* edited by Richard J. Bernstein, pp. 176–98. New York: Liberal Arts Press, 1960.

_____. *Reconstruction in Philosophy.* Boston: Beacon Press, 1957.

Dye, James Wayne. "Heraclitus and the Future of Process Philosophy." In *Tulane Studies in Philosophy 23: Studies in Process Philosophy,* edited by R. C. Wittemore, pp. 13–31. The Hague: Martinus Nijhoff, 1974.

Eames, S. Morris. "Meaning, Value, and Creativity in Dewey and Wieman." In *Creative Interchange,* edited by John A. Broyer and William S. Minor, pp. 208–31. Carbondale: Southern Illinois Univ. Press, 1982.

Farber, Marvin. "Descriptive Philosophy and Human Existence." In *Philosophic Thought in France and the United States,* edited by Marvin Farber, pp. 419–41. Albany: State Univ. of New York Press, 1968.

Fatone, Vicente. *The Philosophy of Nāgārjuna.* Translated by D. Prithipaul. Delhi: Motilal Banarsidass, 1981.

Finch, Leroy. "Introductory Remarks on Nāgārjuna Conference." *Journal of Buddhist Philosophy* 2 (1984): 50–55.

Findlay, J. N. *The Transcendence of the Cave.* London: George Allen and Unwin, 1967.

Fisch, Max H., ed. *Classic American Philosophers.* Englewood Cliffs, N.J.: Prentice-Hall, 1951.

Fox, Richard. *Reinhold Niebuhr.* New York: Pantheon Books, 1986.

Fox, Robin. *Encounter with Anthropology.* New York: Dell, 1968.

Fromm, Erich. *The Heart of Man.* New York: Harper and Row, 1964.

Ganguli, Hemanta Kumar. *Philosophy of Logical Construction.* Calcutta: Sanskrit Pustak Bhandar, 1963.

Geertz, Clifford. "The Impact of the Concept of Culture." In *New Views of the Nature of Man,* edited by John R. Platt, pp. 95–115. Chicago: Univ. of Chicago Press, 1965.

Gilkey, Langdon. "The Mystery of Being and Nonbeing: An Experimental Project." *Journal of Religion* 58 (Jan. 1978): 1–12.

Goldmann, Lucien. *Lukacs and Heidegger: Toward a New Philosophy.* Translated by William Q. Boelhower. London: Routledge and Kegan Paul, 1977.

Govinda, Lama Anagarika. *Creative Meditation and Multi-Dimensional Consciousness.* Wheaton, Ill.: Theosophical Publishing House, 1976.

Grene, Marjorie. *The Knower and the Known.* New York: Basic Books, 1966.

Guenther, Herbert V. *Kindly Bent to Ease Us.* Emeryville, Calif.: Dharma Press, 1975.

_____. *Matrix of Mystery.* Boulder, Colo.: Shambhala, 1984.

_____. *Philosophy and Psychology in the Abhidharma.* Berkeley: Shambhala, 1974.

_____. "Tasks Ahead." Presidential address, Third Conference of the International Association of Buddhist Studies, Winnipeg, Canada, August 1980. *Journal of the International Association of Buddhist Studies* 4 (1981): 115–23.

Guillain, Robert. *The Japanese Challenge.* Translated by Patrick O'Brian. New York: J. B. Lippincott, 1970.

Hall, Edward T. *Beyond Culture.* Garden City, N.Y.: Doubleday, Anchor Books, 1977.

Hall, Stephen S. "Brain Branches Out." *Science 85* 6 (June 1985): 72–74.

Hardwick, Charles S., ed. *Semiotic and Significs: The Correspondence Between Charles S. Peirce and Victoria Lady Welby.* Bloomington: Indiana Univ. Press, 1977.

Hartshorne, Charles. *Creative Synthesis and Philosophic Method.* LaSalle, Ill.: Open Court, 1970.

_____. *Creativity in American Philosophy.* Albany: State Univ. of New York Press, 1984.

_____. "Emptiness and Fullness in Asiatic and Western Thought," *Journal of Chinese Philosophy* 6 (1979): 411–20.

_____. *Insights and Oversights of Great Thinkers: An Evaluation of Western Philosophy.* Albany: State Univ. of New York Press, 1984.

_____. "Introduction: The Development of Process Philosophy." In *Philosophers of Process*, edited by Douglas Browning, pp. v–xxii. New York: Random House, 1965.

_____. *The Logic of Perfection.* LaSalle, Ill.: Open Court, 1962.

_____. Review of *Plato's Philosophy of History*, by Daniel A. Dombrowski. *Process Studies* 12 (Fall 1982): 200–205.

_____. "The Structure of Givenness." *Philosophical Forum* 18 (1960–61): 22–39.

_____. "Toward a Buddhisto-Christian Religion." In *Buddhism and American Thinkers*, edited by Kenneth K. Inada and Nolan Pliny Jacobson, pp. 2–13. Albany: State Univ. of New York Press, 1984.

_____. "Whitehead's Differences from Buddhism." *Philosophy East and West* 25 (Oct. 1975): 407–13.

_____. *Whitehead's Philosophy: Selected Essays, 1935–1970.* Lincoln: Univ. of Nebraska Press, 1972.

_____. "Whitehead's Revolutionary Concept of Prehension." *International Philosophical Quarterly* 19 (Sep. 1979): 253–63.

Hartshorne, Charles, John Cobb, Jr., and Lewis S. Ford. "Three Responses to Neville's *Creativity and God*," *Process Studies* 10 (Fall–Winter 1980): 93–110.

Hegel, Georg Wilhelm Friedrich. *Philosophy of History.* Translated by J. Sibree. New York: Dover, 1956.

Heidegger, Martin. *Hegel's Concept of Experience.* Translated by K. R. Dove. New York: Octagon Books, 1983.

_____. "Letter on Humanism." In *Basic Writings*, edited and translated by David Farrell Krell, pp. 193–242. New York: Harper and Row, 1977.

_____. *Nietzsche.* Translated by David Farrell Krell. Vol. 1. New York: Harper and Row, 1979.

_____. *Poetry, Language, and Thought.* Translated by Albert Hofstadter. New York: Harper and Row, 1971.

Heisenberg, Werner. *Physics and Philosophy: The Revolution in Modern Science.* New York: Harper and Bros., 1958.

Hinchman, Lewis P. *Hegel's Critique of the Enlightenment.* Gainesville: Univ. of Florida Press, 1985.

Hofstadter, Albert. Introduction to *Poetry, Language, and Thought*, by Martin Heidegger. Translated by Albert Hofstadter. New York: Harper and Row, 1971.

Hoyle, Fred. *Highlights in Astronomy.* San Francisco: W. H. Freeman, 1975.

Humphreys, Christmas, ed. Vol. 3 of *Encyclopedia of Buddhism.* Colombo, Sri Lanka: Government Press, 1972.

Hu Shih. "The Scientific Spirit and Method in Chinese Philosophy." In *The Chinese Mind*, edited by Charles A. Moore, pp. 104–31. Honolulu: East-West Center Press, 1967.

Hyppolite, Jean. *Genesis and Structure of Hegel's* Phenomenology of Spirit. Translated by Samuel Cherniak and John Heckman. Evanston, Ill.: Northwestern Univ. Press, 1974.

Ikeda, Daisaku. *Buddhism: The First Millennium.* Translated by Burton Watson. Tokyo: Kodansha International, 1977.

Inada, Kenneth K. "The American Involvement with Śūnyatā: Prospects." In *Buddhism and American Thinkers*, edited by Kenneth K. Inada and Nolan Pliny Jacobson, pp. 70–88. Albany: State Univ. of New York Press, 1984.

_____. "The Metaphysics of Buddhist Experience and the Whiteheadian Encounter." *Philosophy East and West* 25 (Oct. 1975): 465–88.

_____. "The Metaphysics of Cumulative Penetration Revisited." *Process Studies* 13 (Summer 1983): 154–58.

_____. *Nāgārjuna: A Translation of His Mūlamadhyamakakārikā with an Introductory Essay.* Tokyo: Hokuseido Press, 1970.

_____. "Nārgārjuna and Beyond." *Journal of Buddhist Philosophy* 2 (1984): 65–76.

_____. "Problematics of the Buddhist Nature of Self." In *Buddhist and Western Philosophy*, edited by Nathan Katz, pp. 267–86. Atlantic Highlands, N.J.: Humanities Press, 1981.

_____. "The Ultimate Ground of Buddhist Purification." In *Proceedings of the Eleventh International Congress of the International Association for the History of Religions*, vol. 1, p. 146. Leiden, Holland: E. J. Brill, 1968.

_____. "Whitehead's 'actual entities' and the Buddha's 'anatman'." *Philosophy East and West* 21 (July 1971): 303–16.

Izutsu, Toshihiko. *Toward a Philosophy of Zen Buddhism.* Teheran: Imperial Iranian Academy of Philosophy, 1977.

Jacobson, Nolan Pliny. *Buddhism and the Contemporary World: Change and Self-Correction*. Carbondale: Southern Illinois Univ. Press, 1983.

_____. *Buddhism: The Religion of Analysis*. London: George Allen and Unwin, 1966. Reprint. Carbondale: Southern Illinois Univ. Press, Arcturus Books, 1970.

_____. *Understanding Buddhism*. Carbondale: Southern Illinois Univ. Press, 1986.

_____. "The Uses of Reason in Religion." *Iliff Review* 15 (Spring 1958): 49–59.

_____. "Whitehead and Buddhism on the Art of Living." *Eastern Buddhist* 8 (Oct. 1975): 7–36.

James, William. *The Varieties of Religious Experience*. New York: Longmans, Green, 1902.

_____. *The Writings of William James*. Edited by John J. McDermott. New York: Random House, Modern Library, 1968.

Jantsch, Erich. *The Self-Organizing Universe: Scientific and Human Implications of the Emerging Paradigm of Evolution*. Oxford: Pergamon Press, 1980.

Jaspers, Karl. *The Great Philosophers*. Edited by Hannah Arendt. Translated by Ralph Manheim. New York: Harcourt, Brace and World, 1957.

Johanson, Donald, and Maitland Edey. *Lucy: The Beginnings of Mankind*. New York: Simon and Schuster, Warner Books, 1981.

Johansson, Rune E. A. *The Psychology of Nirvana*. London: George Allen and Unwin, 1969.

Kierkegaard, Søren. *Concluding Unscientific Postscript*. Translated by David Swenson. Princeton: Princeton Univ. Press, 1941.

Koller, John M. *Oriental Philosophies*. New York: Charles Scribner's Sons, 1970.

Leach, Edmund. *A Runaway World?* New York: Oxford Univ. Press, 1968.

Leakey, Richard E., and Roger Lewin. *People of the Lake: Mankind and Its Beginnings*. Garden City, N.Y.: Doubleday, Anchor Books, 1978.

Lindtner, Chr. *Nagarjuniana*. Copenhagen: Akademisk Forlag, 1982.

Lowe, Victor, "The Concept of Experience in Whitehead's Metaphysics." In *Alfred North Whitehead: Essays on His Philosophy*, edited by George L. Kline, pp. 124–33. Englewood Cliffs, N.J.: Prentice-Hall, 1963.

————. *Understanding Whitehead*. Baltimore: Johns Hopkins Univ. Press, 1962.

Magliola, Robert. *Derrida on the Mend*. West Lafayette, Ind.: Purdue Univ. Press, 1984.

Malalasekera, G. P., ed. Volumes 1 and 2 of *Encyclopedia of Buddhism*. Colombo, Sri Lanka: Government Press, 1961, 1966.

Maly, Kenneth, and John Sallis, eds. *Heraclitean Fragments: A Companion Volume to the Heidegger/Fink Seminar*. University, Ala.: Univ. of Alabama Press, 1980.

Marx, Karl. *Capital: A Critique of Political Economy*. Translated by Samuel Moore and Edward Aveling. Vol. 1. Chicago: Charles H. Kerr, 1906.

————. "On the Jewish Question." In *The Marx Engels Reader*, edited by Robert C. Tucker, pp. 24–51. New York: W. W. Norton, 1972.

Matson, Wallace. "From Water to Atoms: The Triumph of Metaphysics." In *Language and Thought in Early Greek Philosophy*, edited by Kevin Robb, pp. 255–65. Monist Library of Philosophy. LaSalle, Ill.: Hegeler Institute, 1983.

Matsunaga, Alicia. *The Buddhist Philosophy of Assimilation*. Tokyo: Charles E. Tuttle and Sophia University, 1969.

Meyer, Jeffrey. "Could Buddhist Insights Shape a Better World?" *Charlotte Observer*, Mar. 18, 1984.

Miller, David Lee. "Buddhist Themes in Wieman's View of Creative Interchange." In *Creative Interchange*, edited by John A. Broyer and William S. Minor, pp. 401–20. Carbondale: Southern Illinois Univ. Press, 1982.

————. *Philosophy of Creativity*. Forthcoming.

Miller, J. Hillis. *The Disappearance of God: Five Nineteenth-Century Writers*. Cambridge: Harvard Univ. Press, 1976.

Minor, William S. *Creativity in Henry Nelson Wieman*. Metuchen, N.J.: Scarecrow Press, 1977.

Murti, T. R. V. *The Central Philosophy of Buddhism*. 2d ed. London: George Allen and Unwin, 1960.

Murty, K. Satchidananda. *Nāgārjuna.* New Delhi: National Book Trust, 1971.

Myrdal, Gunnar. *Asian Drama: An Inquiry into the Poverty of Nations.* 3 vols. New York: Twentieth Century Fund, 1968.

Nakamura, Hajime. *Indian Buddhism.* Osaka: Kansai Univ. of Foreign Studies, 1980.

_____. "The Individual and the Universal." In *The Japanese Mind: Essentials of Japanese Philosophy and Culture,* edited by Charles A. Moore, pp. 179–200. Honolulu: East-West Center Press, 1967.

Ñānananda, Bhikkhu. *Concept and Reality in Early Buddhist Thought.* Kandy, Sri Lanka: Buddhist Publication Society, 1971.

Needham, Joseph. *Science and Civilization in China.* 7 vols. Cambridge: Cambridge Univ. Press, 1954.

Niebuhr, Reinhold. *The Nature and Destiny of Man.* 2 vols. New York: Charles Scribner's Sons, 1943.

Nietzsche, Friedrich. *The Birth of Tragedy.* Translated by F. Golffing. Garden City, N.Y.: Doubleday, 1956.

_____. *Philosophy and Truth: Selections from Nietzsche's Notebooks of the Early 1870s.* Edited and translated by Daniel Breazeale. Atlantic Highlands, N.J.: Humanities Press, 1979.

Nishida, Kitarō. "Affective Feeling." In *Japanese Phenomenology: Philosophy as a Transcultural Approach.* Edited by Yoshihiro Nitta, Hirotaka Tatematsu, and Eiichi Shimomissē. Dordrecht, Holland: D. Reidel, 1979.

_____. *Fundamental Problems of Philosophy.* Translated by David Dilworth. Tokyo: Sophia Univ., 1970.

_____. *Intelligibility and the Philosophy of Nothingness.* Translated by Robert Schinzinger. Honolulu: East-West Center Press, 1966.

_____. "The Problem of Japanese Culture." Translated by Masao Abe. In *Sources of Japanese Tradition,* edited by R. Tsunoda, W. T. de Bary, and Donald Keene, pp. 223–47. New York: Columbia Univ. Press, 1958.

Northrop, F. S. C. *Man, Nature, and God.* New York: Simon and Schuster, 1962.

Ohe, Seizo. "Japan in a World-Historical Perspective." *Revue Internationale de Philosophie* 28 (1974): 30–42.

_____. "Scientific Creativity in Eastern Cultural Setting." *Annals of the Japanese Association for Philosophy of Science* 5 (Mar. 1979): 51–56.

Panikkar, Raymond. "The 'crisis' of Mādhyamika and Indian Philosophy Today." *Philosophy East and West* 16 (1966): 117–31.

Peirce, Charles Sanders. *Charles Sanders Peirce: Contributions to the* Nation: *Part Two, 1894–1900.* Compiled by Kenneth Laine Ketner and James Edward Cook. *Graduate Studies 16.* Lubbock: Texas Tech University, 1978.

_____. *Collected Papers of Charles Sanders Peirce.* Vols. 1–6 edited by Charles Hartshorne and Paul Weiss; vols. 7 and 8 edited by A. W. Burke. Cambridge: Harvard Univ. Press, 1931–1935, 1958.

Piguet, J. Claude. *De l' Esthétique à la Métaphysique.* The Hague: Martinus Nijhoff, 1959.

Popper, Karl. *The Logic of Scientific Discovery.* New York: Harper and Row, 1959; Torchbook, 1965.

_____. *The Open Society and Its Enemies.* 5th ed. 2 vols. Princeton: Princeton Univ. Press, 1966.

Potter, Karl. *Presuppositions of India's Philosophies.* Westport, Conn.: Greenwood Press, 1977.

Prigogine, Ilya. *From Being to Becoming.* San Francisco: W. H. Freeman, 1979.

Puligandla, R. *Fundamentals of Indian Philosophy.* Lanham, Md.: Univ. Press of America, 1985.

Radhakrishnan, S. *Indian Philosophy.* 2 vols. London: George Allen and Unwin, 1923, 1927.

Ramanan, K. Venkata. *Nāgārjuna's Philosophy: As Presented in the Mahā-Prajñāparamitā-Sāstra.* Tokyo: Charles E. Tuttle for Harvard-Yenching Institute, 1962.

Reale, Giovanni. *Systems of the Hellenistic Age.* Edited and translated by John R. Catan. Vol. 3 of *A History of Ancient Philosophy.* 3 vols. Albany: State Univ. of New York Press, 1985.

Robb, Kevin. "Preliterate Ages and the Linguistic Art of Heraclitus." In *Language and Thought in Early Greek Philosophy,* edited by Kevin Robb, pp. 153–206. Monist Library of Philosophy. LaSalle, Ill.: Hegeler Institute, 1983.

Rorty, Richard. *Philosophy and the Mirror of Nature.* Princeton: Princeton Univ. Press, 1979.

Rosenblatt, Roger. *Children of War*. Garden City, N.Y.: Double-day, Anchor Books, 1983.

Rosenthal, Sandra B. "Meaning as Habit: Some Systematic Implications of Peirce's Pragmatism." In *The Relevance of Charles Peirce*, edited by Eugene Freeman, pp. 321–28. Monist Library of Philosophy. LaSalle, Ill.: Hegeler Institute, 1983.

Rostovtzeff, M. *The Social and Economic History of the Roman Empire*. New York: Oxford Univ. Press, 1926.

Ryle, Gilbert. *The Concept of the Mind*. New York: Barnes and Noble, 1949.

Santayana, George. "The Two Idealisms: A Dialogue in Limbo." In *The Process of Philosophy*, edited by Joseph Epstein and Gail Kennedy, pp. 497–514. New York: Random House, 1967.

Schrader, George. "The Philosophy of Existence." In *The Philosophy of Kant and Our Modern World*, edited by Charles W. Hendel, pp. 27–64. New York: Liberal Arts Press, 1957.

Sharma, Chandradhar. *Dialectic in Buddhism and Vedānta*. Banaras, India: Nand Kishore and Bros., 1952.

Sheridan, Alan. *Michel Foucault: The Will to Truth*. London: Tavistock, 1980.

Sibatani, Atuhiro. "The Japanese Brain." *Science 80* 1 (Dec. 1980): 22–27.

Singer, Milton. *Man's Glassy Essence: Explorations in Semiotic Anthropology*. Bloomington: Indiana Univ. Press, 1984.

Smart, Ninian. *Doctrine and Argument in Indian Philosophy*. London: George Allen and Unwin, 1964.

Sophocles. *Philoctetes*. In *Ten Greek Plays in Contemporary Translations*, edited by L. R. Lind, translated by Kathleen Freeman, pp. 160–210. Boston: Houghton Mifflin, 1957.

Sperry, Roger. *Values: Number One Problem of Our Times*. New York: Columbia Univ. Press, 1983.

Sprung, Mervyn, ed. *The Question of Being*. University Park, Pa.: Penn State University Press, 1978.

Stcherbatsky, T. I. *The Central Conception of Buddhism and the Meaning of the Word 'Dharma'*. Calcutta: Susil Gupta, 1956. Reprint. Delhi: Indological Book House, 1970.

———. *The Conception of Buddhist Nirvana*. Leningrad: Publishing Office of the Academy of Sciences, USSR, 1927.

Takakusu, Junjirō. *The Essentials of Buddhist Philosophy.* Edited by Wing-tsit Chan and Charles A. Moore. Westport, Conn.: Greenwood Press, 1975.

Tatarkiewicz, Wladyslaw. *History of Aesthetics.* Edited by J. Harrell. 3 vols. Warsaw: PWN–Polish Scientific Publishers; The Hague: Mouton, 1970.

Toynbee, Arnold J. *Civilization on Trial.* New York: Oxford Univ. Press, 1948.

Urmson, J. O. *Philosophical Analysis: Its Development Between the Two World Wars.* New York: Oxford Univ. Press, 1967.

Verdu, Alfonso. *The Philosophy of Buddhism.* The Hague: Martinus Nijhoff, 1981.

Vogel, Ezra. *Japan as Number One.* Cambridge: Harvard Univ. Press, 1979.

Waelhens, Alphonse de. "Notes on Some Trends in Contemporary Philosophy." *Diogenes* 5 (Winter 1959): 39–56.

Walleser, M. *The Life of Nāgārjuna from Tibetan and Chinese Sources.* Delhi: Asia Major, 1923.

Warder, A. K. "Is Nāgārjuna a Mahāyānist?" In *The Problem of Two Truths in Buddhism and Vedānta,* edited by Mervyn Sprung, pp. 78–88. Dordrecht, Holland: D. Reidel, 1973.

Wayman, Alex. "Who Understands the Four Alternatives of the Buddhist Texts?" *Philosophy East and West* 27 (Jan. 1977): 3–21.

Welbon, Guy Richard. *The Buddhist Nirvana and Its Western Interpreters.* Chicago: Univ. of Chicago Press, 1968.

Whitehead, Alfred North. *Adventures of Ideas.* New York: Macmillan, 1933.

_____. *The Aims of Education and Other Essays.* New York: Macmillan, 1929.

_____. *Essays in Science and Philosophy.* New York: Philosophical Library, 1948.

_____. *The Function of Reason.* Boston: Beacon Press, 1958.

_____. *Modes of Thought.* New York: Free Press, 1966.

_____. *The Philosophy of Alfred North Whitehead.* Edited by P. A. Schilpp. New York: Tudor, 1941.

_____. *Process and Reality.* Edited by David Ray Griffin and Donald Sherburne. New York: Free Press, 1978.

_____. *Religion in the Making.* Cleveland: World, 1926.

_____. *Science and the Modern World.* New York: Macmillan, 1925.

_____. *Science and Philosophy.* New Student Outline Series. Paterson, N.J.: Littleford, Adams, 1964.

Whorf, Benjamin Lee. *Language, Thought, and Reality: Selected Writings of Benjamin Lee Whorf.* Edited by J. B. Carroll. Cambridge: MIT Press, 1956.

Wieman, Henry Nelson. *The Directive in History.* Glencoe, Ill.: Free Press, 1949.

_____. *The Empirical Theology of Henry Nelson Wieman.* Edited by Robert Bretall. Library of Living Theology, vol. 4. New York: Macmillan, 1963. Reprint. Carbondale: Southern Illinois Univ. Press, 1969.

_____. "Intellectual Autobiography." Southern Illinois Univ. Archives, Carbondale, Ill.

_____. *Man's Ultimate Commitment.* Carbondale: Southern Illinois Univ. Press, 1958.

_____. "Science and a New Religious Reformation." *Zygon* 1 (June 1966): 125–39.

_____. *The Source of Human Good.* Chicago: Univ. of Chicago Press, 1946. Reprint. Carbondale: Southern Illinois Univ. Press, 1964.

_____. *The Wrestle of Religion with Truth.* New York: Macmillan, 1927.

Wieman, Henry Nelson, and Regina Wescott-Wieman. *Normative Psychology of Religion.* New York: Thomas Y. Crowell, 1935.

Williams, Donald Cary. "Probability, Induction, and the Provident Man." In *Philosophic Thought in France and the United States,* edited by Marvin Farber, pp. 525–43. Albany: State Univ. of New York Press, 1968.

Wittgenstein, Ludwig. *Culture and Value.* Edited by G. H. Von Wright. Translated by Peter Winch. Chicago: Univ. of Chicago Press, 1980.

_____. *Philosophical Investigations.* Translated by G. E. M. Anscombe. Oxford: Basil Blackwell and Mott, 1958.

_____. *Philosophische Bemerkungen.* Edited by Rush Rhees. Oxford: Basil Blackwell and Mott, 1965.

_____. *Tractatus Logico-Philosophicus*. London: Routledge and Kegan Paul, 1949.

Wolfson, Harry Austryn. *Studies in the History of Philosophy and Religion*. Edited by Isadore Twersky and George H. Williams. Cambridge: Harvard Univ. Press, 1973.

Wordsworth, William. *Prelude*. Book 10.

Wriggins, W. Howard. *Ceylon: Dilemma of a New Nation*. Princeton: Princeton Univ. Press, 1960.

Yabuuti, Kiyosi. "The Pre-History of Modern Science in Japan: The Importation of Western Science During the Tokugawa Period." In *Cahiers d'Histoire Mondiale* 9 (1965): 208–32.

# Name Index

# Subject Index

Absolute, 5, 6, 45, 49, 50, 66, 67, 79

Abstraction, 18–19, 26; and Ancient Greeks, 39, 42, 43; conservative function of, 7; and forms of forgetting, 7; Guenther on, 67; Hartshorne on, 23–24; Hegel on, 44; as not freely chosen by individuals, 28; philosophers as critics of, 27; Ramanan on, 2; return from, 32–33, 111; the self as, 37; in Western philosophy, 40, 45, 47, 49, 50–53; Wordsworth on, 44. *See also* Belief systems; Feeling; Individualized experience; Language; Momentary *now*; Original experience; Pure experience; Quality

Advaita Vedanta, 65, 66, 67, 75, 76

Aesthetic foundations of the world, 2, 8, 10, 11; and Hartshorne, 109, 111; and nirvana, 1; and Peirce, 53; Whitehead on, 1, 83. *See also* Concreteness; Individualized experience; Momentary *now*; Quality

Alienation, 12, 47–52, 55–57, 85–86, 109

American civilization: and discovery of concreteness in life, 31–32; and search for new cultural identity, 4–6

American process philosophy: as agent of a new American revolution, 27; and anticipation by philosophies of the West, 25; and experience, 32–33; and Dewey, 1–5; as result of concurrence of three events, 24; and return of individuals from abstraction, 32–33, 111; summarized, 23–25, 28, 30–31; and Whitehead, 1–5. *See also* Process philosophy

Analytical philosophy: broader scope of, in Buddhism, 53–54; late rise of, in Western thought, 52–53

*Anattā* (denial of bifurcating substantial self), ix, 4, 23–24; as affirmed in Buddhism, 68; Hartshorne on, 109; Nakamura on, 68; Naranjo on, 125. *See also Śūnyatā; Svabhāva*

*Aṅguttara-Nikaya,* 17

*Anicca* (transitoriness of life), 62, 114. *See also* Momentariness; Process philosophy

Anxiety: in Kant, 48; and relation to abstractions, 10, 48, 91, 114

Aristotelian-Thomist thought, xii; concept of God in, 40–41; and

Nolan Pliny Jacobson was educated at the University of Wisconsin, Emory University (B.Ph. and B.D.), and the University of Chicago (Ph.D.). After a long and distinguished career teaching the philosophy of religion and American and Asian philosophies at state universities in Florida, North Carolina, Oregon, and Wisconsin, he is now Emeritus Professor of Philosophy and Religion at Winthrop College. Professor Jacobson's work has appeared in several languages in professional journals published in Banaras, Bangkok, London, Moradabad, Paris, Singapore, and Tokyo; he has also had articles in more than a dozen journals based in the United States. His *Nihon-do: The Japan Way* was published in Japanese by Risosha of Tokyo; his *Buddhism: The Religion of Analysis, Buddhism and the Contemporary World: Change and Self-Correction*, and *Understanding Buddhism* are available from Southern Illinois University Press.